LDS Guide
to Scouting in the Primary
Cub Scouts
and
Eleven Year Old
Boy Scouts

Joanne Osmond, jo@LDS-Scouting.org 847.356.7550
Reference: 2011 Scouting Handbook for Church Units in the United States,

This is not an official publication of the Church of Jesus Christ of Latter-day Saints or the Boy Scouts of America.

LDS Guide to Scouting in the Primary

This publication is designed to provide accurate and authoritative information in regard to the subject matter covered. This is not an official publication of the Church of Jesus Christ of Latter-day Saints or the Boy Scouts of America.

Written and compiled from multiple internet sources by Joanne Osmond after the release of the June 2011 version of **Scouting Handbook for Church Units in the United States.**
Copyright © 2011 by Joanne H. Osmond

Published by The Vision Tree, Inc.
216 Waterbury Circle, Lake Villa, IL 60046
Jo@TheVisionTree.com
847.356.7550
Printed in the United States of America
ISBN: 978-1-933334-25-7

More information is available on www.LDS-Scouting.org

LDS Guide to Scouting in the Primary

The purpose of this guide is to:
- Provide leaders and parents with Cub Scout and Eleven-Year-Old Scout specific training in the framework of the Church of Jesus Christ of Latter-day Saint policies and guidelines as published in June 2011.
- Explain the unique aspects of the Scouting program in the LDS Church.

This is an evolving document so please provide feedback and offer recommendations for additions and changes. Forms and documents can be posted on www.LDS-Scouting.org. A healthy dialog is essential in providing the best possible program for the boys in the Church of Jesus Christ of Latter-day Saints. Many thanks to everyone who contributed ideas and recommendations for changes to previous versions including Felicia Brandt (Libertyville, IL), Jennifer Espino (Liberty, Ohio), Tasha Kelley (New Palestine, Indiana), Margo Meade (Portland, Oregon), John and Laurel Osmond (Waukesha, Wisconsin), Kim Sites (Woodstock, IL), Kacey Capps, Paul and Esther Duhacek (Milwaukee, WI), Bud Osmond, and Lake Villa Illinois Pack 174 parents and leaders (Andrea Hunsaker, Scott Lawrence, and Claudia Appel). The Boy Scout information was contributed by the Buffalo Grove Stake LDS Relationships Committee including Ron Peterson, Burt Lowry, Brad Rule, David Allred, Todd Cook, Ken Dewitt, Joe McGrath, and Pat Kitchen.

Resources included:
- Scouting Handbook for Church Units in the United States, June 2011
- Scouting & the Church of Jesus Christ of Latter-day Saints, 2011
- Church Handbook of Instructions, "Aaronic Priesthood", 2010
- Church Handbook of Instructions, "Primary", 2010
- www.lds.org

Additional guides may be purchased through Amazon or sections of the guide can be downloaded from www.LDS-Scouting.org. Copies of this guide may be made and distributed as needed to train Scout parents and leaders.

LDS Guide to Scouting in the Primary

The Cub Scout Monthly Guides and EYOS Monthly Meetings can be downloaded from www.lds-scouting.org.

LDS Guide to Scouting in the Primary

Table of Contents

Scouting in the LDS Church
- Scouting in the Church 9
- Priesthood Purpose 10
- Scouting in an LDS Ward 11
- Faith in God 12
- Adult Religious Award 12
- LDS Scouting Basics 13
- Character Development 16

Advancement
- Cub Scout Advancements 19
- Boy Scout Advancements 25
- Scouting for Eleven-Year-Olds 26
- Uniforms 27

Scouting Organization
- Boy Scouts of America 31
- Unit Organization 33
- Scout Leader Responsibilities 35
- Volunteer Leadership 39
- Scout Training 40
- Training Awards 43

Funding
- Funding 47
- Church Policies 48

Cub Scout Program
- Cub Scout Den 53
- Cub Scout Pack 56
- Flag Ceremony 57
- Scouting Activities 63
- Especially for Parents 65
- LDS Program Planning 66
- Cub Scout Monthly Guides 79

Eleven-Year-Old Program
- Scouting for Eleven-Year-Olds 139
- EYOS Program 140
- Trail to First Class 143
- Troop Guides 144
- Aaronic Priesthood Support 145
- Official BSA Policies 146
- Boy Scout Aims 147
- Troop Advancement Goals 148
- Record Keeping 149
- EYOS Activities 150
- EYOS Monthly Meeting Plans 155

Summary 169

LDS Guide to Scouting in the Primary

Scouting in the LDS Church

Scouting in the Church of Jesus Christ of Latter-day Saints

Since 1910, the BSA has woven lifetime values into fun and educational activities designed to assist parents in strengthening character, good citizenship, and physical fitness in youth. The Church of Jesus Christ of Latter-day Saints has been a sponsoring organization of the BSA since 1913. Why?

"Since in 1913, we became the first partner to sponsor Scouting in the United States. We have remained strong and firm in our support of this great movement for boys and of the Oath and the Law which are at its center. To commit a boy to do his best—to do his duty to God, to his country, to his fellowmen, to true principles, and to himself—is to open avenues of vision and direction for him which can be critically important in his life. A young man who understands and is fully committed to the great principles of the Scout Law has his feet firmly planted on a path that can lead to a happy and constructive life. He will qualify for his own self-respect and he will very likely form wholesome relationships with others and will establish an honorable family. Being true to Scout principles will help him in forming a companionship with his Heavenly Father that will strengthen all the other relationships and aspects of life. It is our understanding and belief that Scouting is still strongly centered in these duties and principles, and that there is a determination in its present leadership to strengthen them further. This being true, The Church of Jesus Christ of Latter-day Saints affirms the continued support of Scouting and will seek to provide leadership which will help boys keep close to their families and close to the Church as they develop the qualities of citizenship and character and fitness which Scouting represents." Spencer W. Kimball

President Kimball spoke these words when he received International Scouting's highest honor, the Silver World Award, from Arch Monson president of the Boy Scouts of America. The methods of Scouting provide an effective means whereby boys can learn self-reliance, teamwork, duty to God and country, and respect for the beliefs and convictions of others—all by subscribing to the Scout Oath and Law and supporting it. In this way, they develop a code of ethics and a sense of values by which they pattern their lives.

In November 2001, President Gordon B. Hinckley said, *"I make you a promise that God will not forsake you if you will walk in His paths with the guidance of His commandments. The promise of the Scout Oath and the twelve points of Scout Law prepare young men for the 21st century."*

Keys to the success of Scouting are: 1) understanding the value of Scouting in preparing boys to receive the priesthood and live the gospel principles, 2) parent involvement, and 3) a commitment to Scouting by ward and stake leadership. Unit leaders in Cub Scout, Boy Scout, Varsity, and Venturing need training not only through the Boy Scout training programs but also by Church leaders with a firm foundation of the purpose and potential of Scouting in shaping the lives of boys and young men.

Priesthood Purpose

At twelve boys move into the Young Men and activities fulfill a priesthood purpose. With these priesthood purposes at the core of all activities, the Aaronic Priesthood program is intended to help young men gain a testimony of Jesus Christ, recognize their particular gifts and the Lord's expectations for them, and prepare for worthy receipt of the Melchizedek Priesthood, for missions, for temple marriage, for fatherhood, and for a lifetime of service in the Church. Scouting is a valuable resource for accomplishing many of the objectives outlined for Aaronic Priesthood activities, but leaders should recognize that it may not be the best vehicle for accomplishing some priesthood purposes. Hence, a healthy balance of all seven of the activity areas is not only desirable but essential.

1. Learn the gospel and build testimonies of Jesus Christ.
2. Give welfare and temporal service.
3. Prepare for and give missionary service.
4. Give genealogical and temple service.
5. Strengthen families.
6. Build quorum brotherhood.
7. Activate young men of quorum age.
8. Build proper relationships with young women.
9. Prepare for eternal marriage and fatherhood.
10. Have leadership experiences.
11. Develop talents.

The Aaronic Priesthood purposes help you to:
- Become converted to the gospel of Jesus Christ and live its teachings.
- Serve faithfully in priesthood callings and fulfill the responsibilities of priesthood offices.
- Give meaningful service.
- Prepare and live worthily to receive the Melchizedek Priesthood and temple ordinances.
- Prepare to serve an honorable full-time mission.
- Obtain as much education as possible.
- Prepare to become a worthy husband and father.
- Give proper respect to women, girls, and children.

Duty to God will help Young Men achieve these purposes of the Aaronic Priesthood. The objectives are reached via personalized goals in these areas:
- Spiritual Strength
- Priesthood Duties
- For the Strength of Youth
- Preparing to receive the Melchizedek Priesthood

Each age group has particular focuses in these areas and uses the Learn, Act, Share process to incorporate them into their lives. The Church of Jesus Christ of Latter-day Saints "Duty to God" is not a Scouting religious award. Boy Scouts and adult leaders in Scouting earn the On My Honor religious award and religious knot. Cub Scouts earn the Faith in God award and religious knot.

"Scouting is an excellent program which develops character in young men. I am grateful for the influence of Scouting in my life and the lives of my sons and grandsons."

President James E. Faust

Scouting in the LDS Ward

When a boy turns eight, he becomes a Cub Scout and joins the ward's pack. When he turns eleven, he becomes a Boy Scout in an EYOS (eleven-year-old Scout) patrol that is part of the ward's Boy Scout troop. Boys eight through eleven are in the Church Primary program which provides religious education and activities for children ages eighteen months through eleven. When a boy or a girl turns twelve, he or she "graduates" from Primary and joins either the Young Men or Young Women program. At age twelve, young men can receive the Aaronic Priesthood.

"In Primary, the Faith in God program should be coordinated with Scouting to lay a foundation that prepares a boy to keep his baptismal covenants, better serve his family, and receive the priesthood. Scouting supports boys and their families by giving them an additional opportunity to put into practice the gospel principles they learn at home and in Primary. Parental involvement and help is a key to success in this program. Scouting also provides boys with leadership opportunities and helps them develop habits and attitudes of good citizenship." (Scouting Handbook, page 3)

Cub Scouts and EYOS are the Activity Day programs for boys in the Church of Jesus Christ of Latter-day Saints. In the United States, where Scouting is part of the Church program, boys work on Faith in God along with Cub Scouting. Many of the Cub Scout activities can fulfill requirements for the award. Completion of all activities in the Faith in God guidebook marked with a knot, qualifies a boy for the Scouting religious square knot patch.

Activity days are designed to provide children age eight through eleven with opportunities to work on activities in the Faith in God program. Primary prepares children for baptism and subsequently for the boys to be worthy to receive the Aaronic Priesthood.

"When properly carried out, Cub Scouting is a fun, home-centered activity program. No Scout-sponsored overnight camping should be planned for boys under age eleven. Details for Cub Scout programs are published by the Boy Scouts of America and are available through local BSA Council offices. "Scouting activities and meetings for Primary-age boys are preferably held in the daytime. Scouting meetings may be held at the meetinghouse, in a home, or in an outdoor setting and should open and close with prayer." (Scouting Handbook, page 3)

"Activity days are held no more than twice each month. They may be held at the meetinghouse or in a home. As leaders determine the frequency and location of activity days, they consider the time constraints of the children's families, travel distance and costs, children's safety, and other local circumstances." (Handbook 2, Administering the Church 11.5.2)

Faith in God Award (BSA Religious Award Square Knot)

The religious award is earned as a Bear or Webelos. The boys can receive the square knot as a Bear which completes one of the achievements for the Bear rank to earn the Faith in God square knot. There are additional religious requirements that are completed to earn the Webelos badge. Many of the achievements, electives, and activity badges have an equivalent in the Faith in God program. The Cub Scout program is designed to put in action the gospel principles taught at home and at Church.

Activities from Boy's Faith in God required for Cub Scout Religious Award	Month
Give a family home evening lesson on Joseph's Smith First Vision (see Joseph Smith- History 1:1-20). Discuss how Heavenly Father answers our sincere prayers. (Learning and Living the Gospel)	April
Give an opening and a closing prayer in family home evening or at Primary. Share your feelings about how prayer protects us and helps us to stay close to Heavenly Father and the Savior. (Learning and Living the Gospel)	N/A
Tell a story from the Book of Mormon that teaches about faith in Jesus Christ. Share your testimony of the Savior. (Learning and Living the Gospel)	August
Prepare a pedigree chart with your name and your parents' and grandparents' names. Prepare a family group record for your family and share a family story. Discuss how performing temple work blesses families. (Learning and Living the Gospel)	June
Write a letter to a teacher, your parents, or your grandparents telling them what you appreciate and respect about them. (Serving Others)	December
Write a story, poem, or short play that teaches a principle of the gospel or is about Heavenly Father's creations. (Developing Talents)	April

Activities from the boy's Faith in God can be completed each month. Select activities that correlate with Cub Scout achievements and electives. To complete the Faith in God, eleven-year-old Boy Scouts will need to continue working on the program and complete the Preparing for the Priesthood section in addition to two activities in each of the other sections. Dovetailing Scouting and Faith in God is the topic of a visual presentation is available at www.lds.org/pa/primary/0,18556,,00.html.

Adult Religious Award – On My Honor

1. Be registered and participate in a Church-sponsored Scouting unit.
2. Be at least twenty-one years of age.
3. Served a minimum of three years in the Aaronic Priesthood or Primary.
4. Be thoroughly familiar with the Aaronic Priesthood or Primary program as shown in an interview with the Bishop.
5. Be worthy as shown in an interview with the Bishop.
6. Complete the basic training for Scouting leaders.

It is important that the ward leadership recognize the volunteers and members of the ward who support the Scouting program. Adult leaders should complete the appropriate award form for their positions to receive recognition from the Boy Scouts of America. Different square knot awards are associated with each position.

LDS Scouting Basics

Scouting is an adventure for boys designed to apply the gospel values and principles taught at home and at Church. We learn how to live the principles by doing as well as through example and instruction. When we realize that the Scouting program has an eternal purpose it becomes a faith-filled journey that strengthens the boys, their leaders, and families.

The program consists of activities that the boy completes at home plus what he accomplishes with his den, pack, EYOS patrol, and troop. Working together he earns recognition for the steps he takes on the journey.

The objective of the LDS Cub Scouting and EYOS outlined in this guide is that every boy receives:

- Cub Scout Faith in God religious knot when he is nine years old.
- Preparing for the Priesthood and Faith in God completed when he is eleven.
- Wolf badge within six months of turning eight.
- Bear badge within six months of turning nine.
- Webelos badge within six months of turning ten.
- Arrow of Light before he turns eleven.
- First Class rank by his 12th birthday.

In addition to the achievements and electives the program utilizes:

- Academic and Sports Belt Loops.
- Leave No Trace Cub Scout Award / Annual Summertime Pack Award.
- Other special awards and recognitions.
- Character Connections and the Core Values.

The boy's Cub Scout handbooks are full of fun ideas for the entire family. The program is flexible and as the den and pack leaders become familiar with the requirements and program, they can easily substitute activities to meet the specific needs of the boys in their den and pack.

The program materials included in this guide were written based on assumptions that are typical of Cub Scout units in the Church of Jesus Christ of Latter-day Saints.

- Boys enter Scouting and advance to the successive years on their birthday: Eight → Wolf, Nine → Bear, Ten → Webelos, Eleven → EYOS (eleven-year-old Scouts). When the boy first enters the Cub Scout program, he earns the rank of Bobcat regardless of his age. Once he earns the Bobcat rank he can work on the age appropriate achievements associated with his rank.
- Many LDS packs are small with approximately five to ten boys and EYOS patrols may be even smaller. At some point in time, there may not be any boys working on one of the ranks and it is common for only one boy to be in an age group. All of the Cub Scouts can meet in one room to ensure two-deep leadership at all times.

- Bear and Wolf dens are often combined with Webelos meeting separately but in the same room. Boys can meet together for part of the time then work separately on individual projects. This program offers parallel tracks so boys can work on similar requirements while advancing in their own rank.

- When the ward covers a large geographic area, den meetings may be held at the chapel at the same time that the Young Men and Young Women meet. This provides additional adult leadership in the building and is especially important for EYOS. Often the den meetings are every other week, alternating weeks with the Girl's Activity Days. The meetings may be the same length as the Young Men/Young Women which is generally between an hour and 1½. In this guide are monthly plans that include den activities that are scheduled to cover multiple requirements and fill the extended time. If the den meeting is longer or shorter, the program can easily be adjusted to meet the local needs.

- The cultural hall is shared with the other organizations using the building. An Annual Pack Planning meeting held in the fall allows time to plan events that require the use of the cultural hall so it can be reserved a year in advance. Pinewood derby, Scout dinner, basketball belt loop, and Cub Scout Olympics are a few of the events that may require a larger space than the Primary room.

- Pack meetings are designed to publicly recognize achievements and progress made by the boys. Boys can show their family what they have accomplished through skits, magic shows, displays, and presentations. It is also an opportunity for the entire family to join in the fun. For example, when the pinewood derby is a ward event, everyone in the ward is encouraged to build and race a car. Blue and Gold banquets can be Scout dinners so Cub Scouts observe Boy Scouts receiving their awards and rank advancement. With families and ward leadership present at the Scout dinner, it is a perfect opportunity to recognize adult leaders.

- Parents and families are willing to work on assignments with their son during Family Home Evening and other times when appropriate to strengthen the family. The activities planned for Cub Scouts are fun for the entire family so they are not a burden but an opportunity to grow in the gospel.

District and council events are opportunities to complete requirements and have fun with other Cub Scouts. If the cost is not prohibitive, packs may participate; at other times information may be provided to families so they can participate. Advancement should not be planned assuming boys will attend council or district events. Events such as Webelos Woods or Loop-a-Palooza (to earn belt loops) are opportunities for boys to learn new skills and earn additional awards; however, attendance should not be required.

Boys should have the opportunity to attend day camp every summer. Outdoor activities are an important part of the Scouting program. A fund raiser approved by the bishop may be used to assist the boys in raising money to attend camp.

Do Your Best

In society where boys are often taught that winning is everything, Cub Scouting teaches them to "do their best" and to be helpful to others.

Cub Scouting is a home and neighborhood-centered program designed to support family life for boys from eight-through-ten years old. Each Cub Scout learns to respect God, his home, country, and other people.

The Cub Scout program helps boys:

- Learn and live the gospel.
- Serve others.
- Use the talents Heavenly Father has given them to learn and do good.
- Learn new physical skills through sports, crafts, and games.
- Learn how to get along with others through group activities.
- Reinforce mental skills such as writing and calculating.
- Develop personal independence.
- Work on activities in the Faith in God program.

A Cub Scout den provides boys with a group of boys his own age in which he can earn awards and recognition. In the den, he will also gain a sense of personal achievement for the new skills he learns.

Cub Scouts work to earn the Faith in God award and the Cub Scout Arrow of Light. Boy Scouts in the Aaronic Priesthood work to earn the Duty to God award and to become an Eagle Scout. Both **Duty to God** and Scouting activities teach boys to "be prepared" in "every needful thing." Achieving the Duty to God and Eagle Scout awards are complementary, not competitive.

The Scouting program is not just for boys. It is a family program to help the family grow closer together and return to our Heavenly Father. Fathers participate in the Boy Scout activities to assist their sons in achieving the objectives of the Church and Scouting. When parents actively participate in the Scouting program with their sons, the boys are more likely to succeed and achieve the goals of the Primary, Aaronic Priesthood, and Scouting.

To accomplish the objective, each boy completes assignments at home and in his den and pack meetings. Depending on his age, boys can work on the activities in the Cub Scout handbooks. Boys will have fun doing the activity with the other boys in his pack even if they completed the requirement previously with their family, friends, or at school.

Boys should be encouraged to invite their friends to join them in Cub Scouts. Nonmember youth are treated exactly as members and do not pay dues or registration fees. If the family offers to make a donation it should be graciously accepted.

Character Development

Since its origin, the Scouting program has been an educational experience concerned with values. In 1910, the first activities for Scouts were designed to build character, physical fitness, practical skills, and service. These elements were part of the original Cub Scout program and continue to be part of Cub Scouting today

Character development should extend into every aspect of a boy's life. Cub Scout leaders should strive to use Cub Scouting's 12 core values throughout all elements of the program—service projects, ceremonies, games, skits, songs, crafts, and all the other activities enjoyed at den and pack meetings

Cub Scouting's 12 Core Values

1. **Citizenship:** Contributing service and showing responsibility to local, state, and national communities.
2. **Compassion:** Being kind, considerate, and showing concern for the well-being of others.
3. **Cooperation:** Being helpful and working together with others toward a common goal
4. **Courage:** Being brave and doing what is right regardless of our fears, the difficulties, or the consequences.
5. **Faith:** Having inner strength and confidence based on our trust in God.
6. **Health and Fitness:** Being personally committed to keeping our minds and bodies clean and fit.
7. **Honesty:** Telling the truth and being worthy of trust.
8. **Perseverance:** Sticking with something and not giving up, even if it is difficult.
9. **Positive Attitude:** Being cheerful and setting our minds to look for and find the best in all situations.
10. **Resourcefulness:** Using human and other resources to their fullest.
11. **Respect:** Showing regard for the worth of something or someone.
12. **Responsibility:** Fulfilling our duty to God, country, other people, and ourselves.

Character can be defined as the collection of core values by an individual that leads to moral commitment and action.

Character development should challenge Cub Scouts to experience core values in six general areas:

- God
- World
- Country
- Community
- Family
- Self

Advancement

Cub Scout Advancement

Pack and Boy Scout leaders assist the families in helping the boys advance. Some advancement requirements are done at den meetings but many are completed at home with the family and signed off by Akela (parent, leader, teacher, grandparent, an older sibling, etc.) In eleven-year-old Scouts, most of the activities are done with the patrol, but it is important that parents maintain good records and follow their son's progress.

Parents are advised to keep all Boy Scout advancement records in a safe place. Plastic sheets that hold baseball cards are a good way to organize the pocket cards that boys receive along with their awards. The use of online tracking programs, such as Troopmaster and Packmaster, are effective in managing the boy's records. Parents play an active role in ensuring that the boy's records are up-to-date and accurate.

Bobcat

All boys, ages eight-through-ten, earn the Bobcat Badge by learning the Cub Scout Promise, Law of the Pack, Handshake, Salute, Sign, Motto, and the meaning of "Webelos." After receiving the Bobcat Badge, boys work on requirements based on their age group.

Cub Scout Promise
I, (name), promise to do my best
To do my duty to God and my country,
To help other people,
And to obey the Law of the Pack.

Law of the Pack
The Cub Scout follows Akela.
The Cub Scout helps the pack go.
The pack helps the Cub Scout grow.
The Cub Scout gives goodwill.

Cub Scout Motto
Do Your Best.

Note: Packs chartered by the Church of Jesus Christ of Latter-day Saints do not support a program for boys who are younger than eight-years-old.

Wolf

A Cub Scout who is eight years old is a member of the Wolf den and works on twelve achievements to earn the Wolf badge.

After he earns his Wolf badge, a boy may work on electives in different interest areas until he is nine when he begins work on the next badge. He earns gold and silver Arrow Points as he completes electives.

Planning Tip: For every boy to earn the Wolf badge in their first six months, the twelve achievements are covered twice a year with alternative activities for boys if they have already completed the achievements. Boys are given assignments to complete at home then reviewed by the den leader to reduce redundancy. By covering the twelve achievements twice, boys will start receiving their immediate recognition as soon as possible after their eighth birthday and achieve their Wolf badge in six months.

After the Wolf badge is earned, the electives and extra achievements completed before they received their Wolf badge are used to earn gold and silver Arrow Points. The eight-year-old Scout continues to complete electives and earn Arrow Points until he is nine.

Cub Scout recognition should be timely and include the Immediate Recognition at den meetings as well as patches, pins, and belt loops at pack meetings. The Wolf receives a yellow bead when he has completed three achievements. A Bear receives a red bead when he completes three achievements that he can use towards his Bear badge.

Bear

A Cub Scout who is nine-years-old is a member of the Bear den and works to complete twelve of twenty-four achievements in four areas. Boys complete one achievement in God, three in Country, four in Family, and four in Self to earn the badge. After he earns his Bear badge, a boy may work on electives in different interest areas until he is ten and begins working on the Webelos rank.

Arrow Points

For every ten electives a boy completes, he earns an Arrow Point. A boy may earn Arrow Points after he receives his Wolf or Bear badge until his next birthday when he starts working on his next rank. Requirements completed under an achievement, but not used toward the Wolf badge, can be used as an elective. Achievements not used to earn the Bear badge can be used as an elective; however the unused parts of the achievements that were used for the Bear badge may not be counted toward Arrow Points. For example, Achievement 6, Take Care of Your Planet, has seven requirements but only three are required to complete the achievement. If four of the seven are completed, the extra requirement cannot be used toward an Arrow Point if Achievement 6 is used to achieve the Bear badge. Otherwise all four can be used toward an Arrow Point.

Planning Tip: During the year the achievements are staggered so the boys achieve their Bear badge in six months and continue to work on Arrow Points after receiving their award.

Webelos Overview

When a Cub Scout is ten years old, he transfers to a Webelos den, led by an adult Webelos leader. The boy works on requirements for the Webelos badge, twenty activity badges, and the Arrow of Light (the highest award in Cub Scouts).

Planning Tip: To accommodate small units, the Webelos activity badges (pins) correlate to the monthly Core Value, as well as, the Wolf and Bear activities. One adult leader should never take a boy alone into a room to work on requirements. (Unless of course the leader is the boy's parent.) By combining Cub Scout and Webelos dens, boys can work in the same room on different but similar projects, thus two-deep leadership is easier to maintain.

To earn the Webelos badge, the Cub Scout completes various requirements including three activity badges (Fitness, Citizen, and one other). To earn the Webelos badge the Cub Scout learns the Boy Scout Salute, Sign, Handshake, Oath, Law, Slogan, and Motto plus he fulfils additional religious requirements.

When the boy earns four additional activity badges (total of seven), he can earn the Compass Point emblem. For each additional four activity badges, the Cub Scout can earn a Compass Point. Because the LDS program completes the Webelos badge and Arrow of Light in one year verses two, it is a challenge to earn all of the activity badges. Additionally, many LDS packs do not use the Compass Points as an immediate recognition because of the additional expense.

Webelos activity badges worn on the Tricolor include:

- **Physical Group**: *Fitness*, Aquanaut, Athlete, Sportsman
- **Mental Group**: Artist, Scholar, Showman, Traveler
- **Community Group**: *Citizen*, Communicator, Family Member, *Readyman*
- **Technology Group**: Craftsman, Engineer, Handyman, Scientist
- **Outdoor Group**: Forester, Geologist, Naturalist, *Outdoorsman*

*Italics indicates the four required badges for Webelos and Arrow of Light.

The program outlined in this guide covers *Fitness* and *Citizen* Activity badges twice during the year so a ten year old boy can earn his Webelos badge in his first six months regardless of his birthday.

Activity badge requirements for Webelos badge include:
- *Fitness* (Earned for the Webelos badge)
- *Citizen* (Earned for the Webelos badge)
- One more activity badge (In Mental, Technology, or Outdoor)

After a boy has been active in the Webelos den for six months and has his Webelos badge, he can earn the Arrow of Light award. He must earn a total of eight activity badges including the Fitness, Citizen, Readyman, and Outdoorsman and complete the requirements to be a Boy Scout.

 To earn the Arrow of Light and Outdoorsman activity badge, the Cub Scout can participate in two day hikes, rather than overnight camping.

Note: No Scout-sponsored overnight camping should be planned for boys under eleven years old.

Activity badge requirements for the Arrow of Light include:

- *Readyman*
- *Outdoorsman*
- At least one from Mental Skills Group
- At least one from the Technology Group
- One more of your choice

The Arrow of Light can be worn on his Boy Scout uniform and his adult uniform.

Cub Scout Sports and Academic Program

 Belt loops for the Academic and Sports program are in integral part of the Webelos advancement program. Activities are divided into two categories: Academics and Sports. Each category has many skills and activities from which Scouts may choose. The Cub Scout belt loop and pin program encourages a boy to do his best while learning skills and promoting good sportsmanship.

The sports activity areas include: Archery, BB Gun Shooting, Badminton, Baseball, Basketball, Bicycling, Bowling, Fishing, Flag Football, Fitness, Golf, Gymnastics, Hiking, Hockey, Horseback Riding, Ice Skating, Kickball, Marbles, Roller Skating, Skateboarding, Snow Ski and Board Sports, Soccer, Softball, Swimming, Table Tennis, Tennis, Ultimate, and Volleyball.

The academics activity areas include: Art, Astronomy, Chess, Citizenship, Collecting, Communicating, Computers, Disabilities Awareness, Family Travel, Geography, Geology, Good Manners, Heritages, Language and Culture, Map and Compass, Mathematics, Music, Nutrition, Pet Care, Photography, Reading and Writing, Science, Video Games, Weather, and Wildlife Conservation.

Using the Academic and Sports belt loops and pins may be cost prohibitive. If so, look for an alternative form of recognition, such as, small segment patches, beads, feathers, cards, ribbons, or stickers to track their progress on a chart. The boys can complete the requirements and be recognized without receiving the belt loops and pins sold by the BSA.

Webelos Badge Requirement

1. Parents read and sign Webelos Parent Guide pages 1-22.
2. Be an active member of your Webelos den for 3 months.
3. Know and explain the meaning of the Webelos badge.
4. Point out and explain the three parts of the Webelos Scout uniform. Tell when to wear the uniform and when not to wear it.
5. Earn the *Fitness* and *Citizen* Activity badges and one other activity badge from a different activity badge group.
6. Plan and lead a flag ceremony in your den that includes the U.S. flag.
7. Show that you know and understand the requirements to be a Boy Scout.
    a. Demonstrate the Scout salute, Scout sign, and Scout handshake. Explain when you would use them.
    b. Explain the Scout Oath, Scout Law, Scout motto, and Scout slogan.
    c. Explain and agree to follow the Outdoor Code.
8. Faith
    a. **Know**: Tell what you have learned about faith.
    b. **Commit**: Tell how these faith experiences help you live your duty to God. Name one faith practice that you will continue to do in the future.
    c. **Practice**: After doing these requirements, tell what you have learned about your beliefs.

Do two of these:
    a. Attend the mosque, church, synagogue, temple, or other religious organization of your choice, talk with your religious leader about your beliefs. Tell your family and your Webelos den leader what you learned.
    b. Discuss with your family and Webelos den leader how your religious beliefs fit in with the Scout Oath and Scout Law, and what character-building traits your religious beliefs have in common with the Scout Oath and Scout Law.
    c. With your religious leader, discuss and make a plan to do two things you think will help you draw nearer to God. Do these things for a month.
    d. For at least a month, pray or meditate reverently each day as taught by your family, and by your church, temple, mosque, synagogue, or religious group.
    e. Under the direction of your religious leader, do an act of service for someone else. Talk about your service with your family and Webelos den leader. Tell them how it made you feel.
    f. List at least two ways you believe you have lived according to your religious beliefs.

Outdoor Code

As an American, I will do my best to:
- Be clean in my outdoor manners.
- Be careful with fire.
- Be considerate in the outdoors.
- Be conservation minded.

Arrow of Light Requirements

The highest award in Cub Scouts is earned by Webelos that are active participants in their den and are ready to join a Boy Scout troop. Many of the requirements for the Arrow of Light are intended to familiarize the scout with a local troop and hopefully show him that crossing over into a troop is the next step to take in Scouting. A Scout that earns his Arrow of Light patch has also completed most of the requirements to earn the Scout badge in the troop so he has begun his Boy Scout trail.

1. Be active in your Webelos den for at least six months and has already earned the Webelos badge.
2. Show your knowledge of the requirements to become a Boy Scout by doing all of these:
    - Repeat from memory and explain in your own words the Scout Oath or Promise and the 12 points of the Scout Law. Tell how you have practiced them in your everyday life.
    - Give and explain the Scout motto, slogan, sign, salute, and handshake.
    - Understand the significance of the First Class Scout badge. Describe its parts and tell what each stands for.
    - Tell how a Boy Scout uniform is different from a Webelos Scout uniform.
    - Tie the joining knot (square knot).
3. Earn five more activity badges in addition to the three you already earned for the Webelos badge. These must include:
    - *Fitness* (already earned for the Webelos badge)
    - *Citizen* (already earned for the Webelos badge)
    - *Readyman*
    - *Outdoorsman*
    - At least one from the Mental Skills Group
    - At least one from the Technology Group
    - Two more of your choice
4. With your Webelos den, visit at least:
    - One Boy Scout troop meeting
    - One Boy Scout-oriented outdoor activity. (If you have already done this when you earned your Outdoorsman activity badge, you may not use it to fulfill requirements for your Arrow of Light award.)
5. Participate in a day hike. (Do not count a hike taken to fulfill the requirement for Outdoorsman.
6. Have a conference with the EYOS leader.
7. Complete the Honesty Character Connection.
    a. **Know**: Say the Cub Scout Promise to your family. Discuss: What is a promise? What does it mean to keep your word? What does it mean to be trustworthy? What does honesty mean?
    b. **Commit**: Discuss: Why is a promise important? Why is it important for people to trust you when you give your word? When might it be difficult to be truthful? List examples.
    c. **Practice**: Discuss: Why it is important to be trustworthy and honest. How can you do your best to be honest even when it is difficult?

Boy Scout Advancement

When a boy turns eleven, he completes the Boy Scout application and health form to join the Boy Scout troop. If the new Boy Scout earned the Arrow of Light award, he demonstrates that he knows how to tie a square knot to earn his Scout Badge. If the boy has not received his Arrow of Light, he completes all of the requirements to earn the Scout badge.

Boy Scout Oath
On my honor, I will do my best
To do my duty to God and my country
And to obey the Scout Law;
To help other people at all times;
To keep myself physically strong,
Mentally awake,
And morally straight.

Scout Motto
Be Prepared.

Scout Slogan
Do a Good Turn Daily.

Scout Law
A Scout Is:
Trustworthy
Loyal
Helpful
Friendly
Courteous
Kind
Obedient
Cheerful
Thrifty
Brave
Clean
Reverent

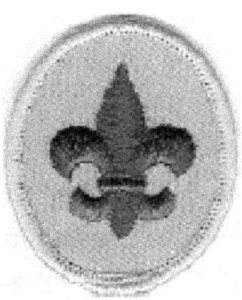

Scouting provides many opportunities for boys to learn skills and take part in outdoor adventures. The Boy Scouts of America recognizes the boy's achievement by awarding badges: Scout, Tenderfoot, Second Class, First Class, Star, Life, and the highest rank of Eagle.

When the Scout is eleven years old, he is a member of the Boy Scout troop but in a special "New-Scout patrol" that focuses on the requirements for the first four ranks. He must earn Scout before he starts working on the next three ranks. He may complete any of the requirements for Tenderfoot, Second Class, and First Class at any time and in any order. An active Scout can earn First Class when he is an EYOS.

Regardless of the requirements the Scout has completed, he receives the ranks in this order.

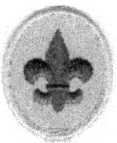 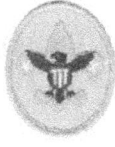   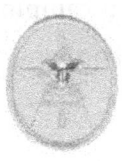  

Scout   Tenderfoot   Second Class   First Class   Star   Life   Eagle

Reminder: It is important to maintain accurate records; they will be used in completing the Eagle application.

Scouting for the Eleven-Year-Old
From www.lds.org (9/2011)

"Scouting is fun and has an important purpose! Woven through all the fun is an inspired program that really works. Scouting is about learning and living the gospel. Scouting can reinforce positive character values and leadership skills that are taught in the home.

"Scouting prepares boys to become righteous men who hold and honor the priesthood of God. Scout leaders have the responsibility to help each boy connect what he is learning in Scouting to his priesthood preparation and his future as a covenant keeping missionary, husband, and father."

Cheryl C. Lant, Primary General President

The work of Scouting is accomplished through weekday activities that are designed to help boys practice skills and learn the practical application of principles taught during Sunday Primary (see Scouting Handbook, page 4).

A newly called leader of the eleven-year-old Scouts should begin by prayerfully coming to understand the importance of this calling within the ward Primary and Scouting organizations and the significance this service can have in the life of a boy. The leader of the eleven-year-old Scouts should:

- Register with the Boy Scouts of America, through the local council.
- Study the Church-published Scouting Handbook (35814) and then participate in Basic Training. To supplement training from local priesthood leaders, the Scout leader may enroll in additional classes to help learn Scouting methods and skills (see Scouting Handbook, 1).
- Serve under the direction of a member of the Primary presidency, meeting together regularly to discuss the Scouting program and each boy's progress.
- Attend ward Primary leadership meetings.
- Supervise patrol meetings and Scouting activities for the eleven-year-old Scouts, encourage each boy to advance in Scouting, and keep an accurate record of his progress.
- See that each Scout has an opportunity to participate in a day camp and help plan it if requested (see A Day Camp Guide for Eleven-Year-Old Scouts, 31374).
- Consult with the ward Primary presidency and the bishopric adviser to the Primary when organizing each overnight camping experience.
- Review the Scouting Handbook for additional information concerning the responsibilities of the Scout leader.

Information is available about the eleven-year-old programs on the www.lds.org web site at www.lds.org/pa/display/0,17884,4834-1,00.html.

LDS Guide to Scouting in the Primary

Scout Uniforms

The Boy Scouts of America utilizes a uniform to create a sense of belonging. The uniform symbolizes character development, citizenship training, and personal fitness. Wearing a uniform gives youth and adult members a sense of identification and commitment. The uniform is easily recognized and respected in the public. On the official Scout web site www.Scouting.org, four points are made about the use of a uniform in Scouting.

- **Personal equality** – The uniform represents a democratic idea of equality, bringing people of different backgrounds together in the Scouting tradition.
- **Identification** – The uniform identifies youth and adult members of the Boy Scouts of America, visible as a force for good in the community. When properly and smartly worn, the uniform can build good unit spirit.
- **Achievement** – The uniform shows the wearer's activity, responsibility, and achievement. The accomplishments of every youth and adult member can be recognized by the insignia worn on the uniform.
- **Personal commitment** – The uniform is a constant reminder to all members of their commitment to the ideals and purpose of the Scouting movement. It is a way of making visible members' commitment to a belief in God, loyalty to country, and helping others.

The leaders of Scouting—volunteer and professional—should promote the wearing of the correct, complete uniform on all suitable occasions.

It is the family's responsibility to purchase the uniform. Officially, Church policy does not approve the purchase of uniforms with Church funds; however *"Units may wish to maintain a supply of used uniforms to make them available for boys. Abbreviated or simple uniforms and insignia, which have been approved by the BSA, are appropriate and encouraged."* (Scouting Handbook, page 6)

The minimum required Cub Scout uniform consists of a blue Cub Scout shirt, neckerchief and slide. A belt is recommended if belt loops are purchased to recognize the requirements for the Academic and Sports program. Webelos can wear either the blue shirt or may replace it with a khakis Boy Scout shirt if he out grows his blue shirt.

Useful Hint: A supply of neckerchiefs (Wolf – yellow, Bear – blue, Webelos – plaid) can be maintained by the pack and brought to den and pack meetings along with an assortment of slides.

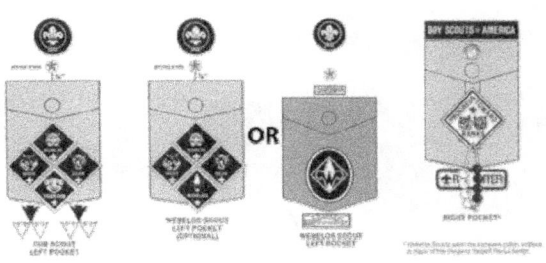
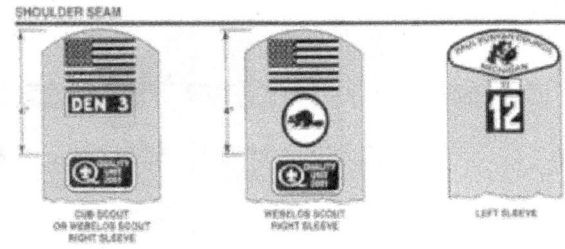

Red Patch Vest

Boys and adults will collect numerous patches at den, pack, district, and council events. One patch can be worn on the right hand pocket of the uniform shirt. To display all of the patches a patch vest (also known as a brag vest) can easily be made. In lieu of a vest, a jacket, blanket, wall hanging, bulletin board, etc. can be made to display the colorful patches including all camporee, day camp, sporting events, derbies, pack outing, hiking, and council sponsored event patches. The Varsity "C" letter can be placed on the vest – academic and sports pin can be placed on the patch. Metals from derbies can be pinned to the vest.

If a red vest is used to hold all the patches the boy receives during his time in Scouts, it is not considered part of the official uniform. The vest is fun to wear when he attends a special event where he can show off his patches to other Scouts. The decision to purchase a vest (or make it) and attach the patches, is left up to the parents of the Scout.

Eleven-Year-Old Scout Uniform

The EYOS wears a khakis uniform shirt with the neckerchief. Note that the World Crest located above the left pocket is worn by all Scouts and leaders to signify membership of our program in the World Scouting movement. This patch shows our brotherhood with millions of Scouts around the world. The World Crest is worn centered above the left pocket in the middle between the top of the pocket and the shoulder seam.

Adult Leader Uniform

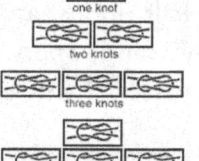

Adult leaders set an example for the boys and wear a uniform and insignia for the position they hold. Cub Scout leaders wear the blue epaulets on a khakis or yellow shirt. Red or olive green epaulets are worn by Boy Scout leaders, orange epaulets by Varsity Team leaders, green by Venturing Crew leaders, and silver by district or council leaders.

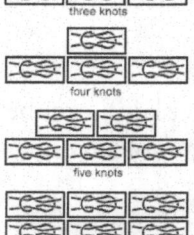

Adult leaders wear knots above their left pocket indicating training awards and other recognitions that they have received. Adult leaders may also wear a brag vest or red jacket where event patches are sewn. A Scout leader who has attended Philmont may sew a white steer on the red jacket.

Arrow of Light | Eagle Scout | Youth Religious Award | Adult Religious Award | Cub Scouter Award | Den Leader Award | Cubmaster Award | Boy Scouter Award | District Award of Merit | Silver Beaver

Scouting Organization

Boy Scouts of America

National Council for the Boy Scouts of America is located in Irving, Texas. The National Council is the corporate membership of the Boy Scouts of America and consists of volunteer Scouters who meet annually. The day-to-day operations of the National Council are administered by the Chief Scout Executive and other national professional staff. National Council members include volunteers who are elected National Officers and Executive Board members, regional presidents, the local council representatives, members at large, and honorary members.

The BSA was granted a Congressional charter in 1916 stating that their purpose is to: promote, through organization, and cooperation with other agencies, the ability of boys to do things for themselves and others, to train them in scoutcraft, and to teach them patriotism, courage, self-reliance, and kindred virtues, using the methods that were in common use by boys.

Regions and Areas

For administrative purposes, the BSA is divided into four regions—Western, Central, Southern and Northeast. Each region is then subdivided into areas. Each region has a volunteer president, assisted by volunteer officers, board members, and committee members. The day-to-day work of Scouting is managed by the regional director, assistant and associate regional directors, and area directors. Regions and areas are subdivisions of the National Council and do not have a corporate status separate from the BSA.

Local Councils

The BSA program is administered through fewer than 300 local councils, with each council covering a geopolitical area that may vary from a single city to an entire state. Councils receive an annual charter from the National Council. The council level organization is similar to that of the National Council. The council executive board is headed by the council president and is made up of annually elected local community leaders. The board establishes the council program and carries out the resolutions, policies, and activities of the council. Board members serve without pay and some are volunteer Scouters working at the unit level.

The Scout executive manages council operations—including finance, property management, membership, advancement and awards, registrations, and Scout Shop sales—with a staff of other professionals and para-professionals. Volunteer Commissioners lead the unit service functions of the council, help maintain the standards of the BSA, and assures a healthy unit program.

Councils are divided into districts with leadership provided by the district director, district chairman, and the district commissioner. Districts are directly responsible for the operation of Scouting units and, except for the district director and executives, are mostly staffed with volunteers. The voting members of each district consist of volunteer representatives from each chartered organization having at least one BSA unit, plus annually elected members-at-large who in turn elect the district chairman.

Chartered Organizations and Units

The Boy Scouts of America partners with community organizations, such as religious congregations, fraternal groups, service clubs, and other community associations, to provide the Scouting program for the particular neighborhood or community in which the particular organization wishes to outreach to youth and families. These organizations hold charters issued by the BSA and are known then as chartered organizations. Each chartered organization provides the meeting place for BSA youth, oversees the volunteer leaders, and agrees to follow the basic BSA safety policies and values-based program, and the organization is considered the "owner" of its local program, much like a franchise.

The Church of Jesus Christ of Latter-day Saints was the first sponsor of the BSA and today contributes the more Scouts than any other chartered organization.

Within each chartered organization, there may be one or more "units". A unit is a group of youth and adults which are collectively designated as a Cub Scout pack, Boy Scout troop, Varsity Scout team, or Venturing crew/Sea Scout ship. Each chartered organization may charter as many units as it wishes, but usually only three or four (one unit for each program level). The BSA council provides the leader training, inter-unit activities, camping programs, volunteer and professional support, and insurance coverage. Units also create their own activities (such as monthly camping trips, outings, or service projects), and most meet weekly at the place of the chartered organization for youth to learn basic skill development and practice leadership in small groups known as dens and patrols.

The staff at the Boy Scout service centers can help or know who to contact to assist the ward.

- Packs can maintain a pack library that contains the leader books to enhance the program activities.

- District roundtable, a monthly leaders' meeting for all adult volunteers in the district, is available. Typically the roundtable provides help with crafts, games, skits, and songs for use at den and pack meetings. It's a great place to ask questions and share ideas.

- Districts have a team of volunteers called the district committee, which develops quality district-wide programs in which boys can participate. The council newsletter and web site contains updated information about the activities planned for Cub Scouts and Boy Scouts.

A unit commissioner is assigned to check on the health of the pack, troop, team, and crew. He or she is a communication link between the unit and the Scouting organization. At the request of the Stake presidency, a member of the stake may be assigned by the district to be the unit commissioner; however a unit commissioner is not a Church calling.

Exploring is a unique career exploration program for young men and women ages 14 – 20 which provides an ideal link between the academic environment and the real world. Learning for Life features grade-appropriate, theme-oriented lesson plans to be used in the classroom to enhance and support the core curriculum.

Unit Organization

The troop, team, and crew are the activity program for the Aaronic Priesthood and are supported by either one Scout committee or multiple committees. Eleven-year-old Scouts (EYOS) constitutes a patrol in the Boy Scout troop, but remain part of the Primary organization. The EYOS leader is a calling in the Primary. The Cub Scout pack is also part of the Primary organization and is supported by a separate pack committee. The pack is made up of den leaders, Cubmaster, the pack trainer, pack committee members, and the Primary presidency with all parents expected to register and adhere to Youth Protection guidelines.

1. The Scout committee may include leadership from the EYOS, troop, team, and crew.
2. A Key Scout Leader meeting including pack, EYOS, troop, team, and crew leadership may meet prior to pack and scout committees.
3. Adult leaders meet once a month, or more often, if needed.
4. The Key Scout Leader meeting is lead by the member of the bishopric responsible for Scouting (Charter Organization Representative or COR). The pack and scout committees are led by a committee chairman called by the bishopric.

The committees select the meeting place and time, perform record keeping, manage finances, order badges and other recognitions, maintain equipment, train leaders, and recognize leaders. (Refer to Scouting Handbook pages 2 – 3 for more information about the ward committee.)

The pack, troop, team, and crew are sponsored by the ward, i.e., "LDS Lake Villa 1 Ward, Buffalo Grove Illinois Stake."

"Chartering of Cub packs, Boy Scout troops, Varsity teams, and Venturing crews is done annually. Each ward registers its own Cub pack, eleven-year-old Scout patrol, Boy Scout troop, Varsity team, and, when sponsored, Venturing Crew. Stakes do not charter stake Scouting units."

"Combining activities for small units during the week may be authorized by the stake president, so long as each ward maintains a properly registered unit; each is staffed with adult leaders; and retention, recruitmen and activation efforts are maintained by each ward or quorum." (Scouting Handbook, page 5)

Please note that the Church does not sponsor a Scouting program for girls or Young Women. Community Venturing crews may be co-ed and outside the United States Scouting is often for boys and girls. The Activity Day program and Young Women are designed to meet the needs of the girls and young women in the ward.

Ward Leader Responsibilities

The charter organization for Scout units is the ward (not the stake).

Parents are key to a high-functioning committee. They fulfill many of the tasks that support the Scouting program and the leaders. With the parent's assistance, their boys will advance and achieve the purposes of Scouting and the Church.

LDS Guide to Scouting in the Primary

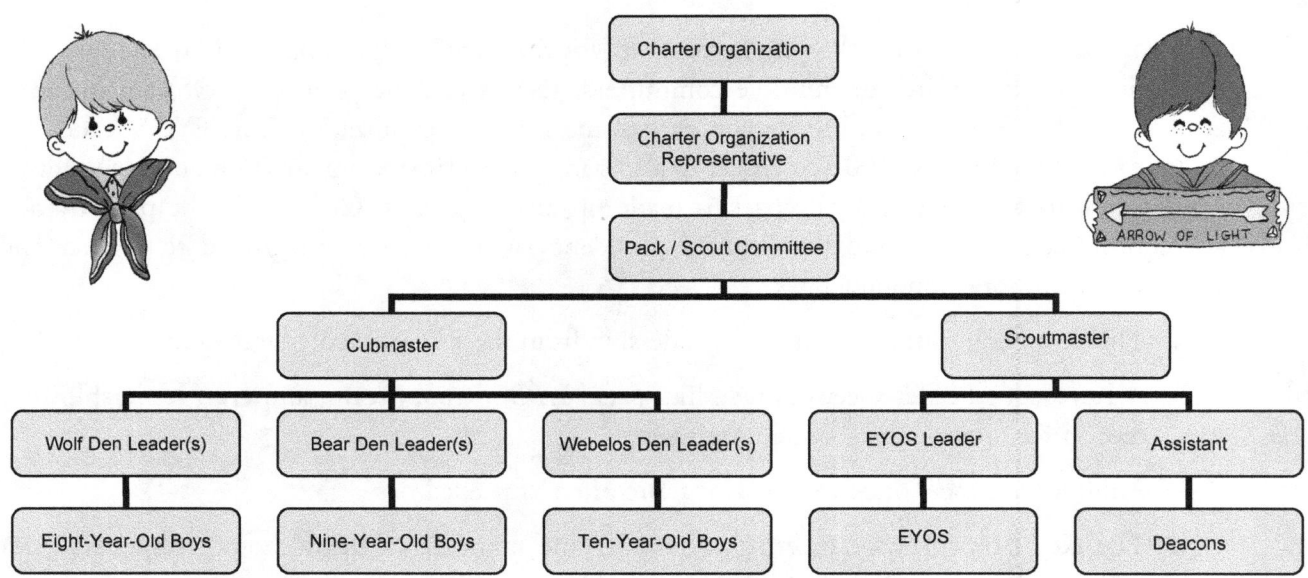

Pack / Troop Committee
Pack and troop committees perform the administrative functions of the pack and troop.

Committee Chairman
Called by bishopric. Presides at leader's committee meetings. Helps recruit and recommend adult leaders. Attends the pack meeting / court of honor.

Advancement Chairman
Maintains advancement records for the pack / troop. Obtains all badges and insignia. Attends pack meetings / courts of honor and committee meetings.

Pack Trainer
Coordinates "Fast Start" Training for adults, organizes the dens, and promotes leader training and roundtable attendance. Can be a member of the Primary presidency.

Secretary / Treasurer
Keeps all records for the unit, coordinates financial records with ward clerk. Attends pack / troop meetings and leaders' committee meetings.

Safety Coordinator
Responsible to ensure safety standards are followed. Ensures Youth Protection is a unit priority.

Scoutparents Coordinator
Welcomes families and coordinates their participation on committees. Activity chairman to coordinate "one shot" program jobs and Scouting for Food, Friends of Scouting, pinewood derby, Scout banquet, day camp, transportation, etc. These jobs are of short duration.

Den Leader
Called by bishopric. Leads the den at den and pack meetings. Attends committee meetings.

Cubmaster / Scoutmaster
Called by bishopric. Helps plan and carry out the program with the help of the committee. Emcees pack meeting / courts of honor.

To provide a quality program, Scout units need everyone.

Scout Leader Responsibilities

When members are called to Scout leader positions they are set apart. Non-members can receive a blessing. Parents are encouraged to volunteer to assist in pack and den activities and should register with the BSA as a committee member. It is only through the efforts of dedicated parents that the organization runs smoothly. It is also critical to ensure that there are qualified adults to provide two-deep leadership when transporting youth to the Church or to activities.

- Qualified adults, whether members of the Church or not, may hold Scouting positions. All must maintain the Church standards.
- The bishopric approves and calls leadership and keeps the unit within LDS and Boy Scout standards and policies.
- Where leadership is limited, one committee may be called to service all Scouting needs for the young men and another for the Cub Scouts.
- *"Each committee should include a member of the bishopric."* (Scouting Handbook, page 2)
- Men and women can serve in Scout positions for Primary age boys (Cub Scouts and eleven-year-old Scouts) but only men are called to serve boys who are in Aaronic Priesthood age groups. Women can serve as the chair of the Scout committee.

"When more than one Scouting committee exists in the ward, members of the Primary presidency should be assigned as follows: (1) the member responsible for the eleven-year-old boys serves on the Boy Scout troop committee and (2) the member responsible for eight-, nine-, and ten-year-old Scouting serves on the Cub Scout pack committee." (Scouting Handbook, page 3)

The purpose of the committee is to support and assist Scouting activities by providing service to the units and to see that the units are operating in accordance with both the Church and the BSA policies and standards. The Boy Scouts of America requires that ALL Scout leaders take Youth Protection training, available at www.scouting.org prior to working with boys or young men. The training must be taken every two years.

"Two registered adult leaders or one registered adult leader and a parent of a participant (one of whom must be 21 years of age or older) are required on all Scouting trips, outings, classes, and meetings. In situations that require personal conferences, such as a Scoutmaster's conference or merit badge counseling, the meeting must be conducted in view of other adults or youth. When camping, no youth is permitted to sleep in the tent of an adult other than his own parent or guardian. Adult leaders must respect the privacy of youth in situations such as changing clothes and taking showers at camp, and intrude only when health and safety require doing so. Adults should also protect their own privacy in similar situations." (Scouting Handbook, page 5)

"The Boy Scouts of America will complete a criminal background check on all new adult leaders as part of the registration approval process. This will include the screening of Social Security numbers. Priesthood leaders should cooperate with BSA officials to resolve any issues that arise and complete this process before sustaining and setting apart each Scout leader." (Scouting Handbook, page 6)

Bishop's Role

"The bishop provides general direction for Scouting in the ward and ensures that it is properly organized and functioning as outlined in the Scouting Handbook and Handbook 2 (8.13, 11.5). He is registered and serves as the executive officer for Scouting units chartered by the ward." (Scouting Handbook, page 2)

Bishopric's Responsibilities

The bishopric counselors help the bishop by ensuring that the Scouting program for Primary age boys and the Aaronic Priesthood are functioning. The Charter Organization Representative (COR) is the member of the bishopric responsible for Scouting. The Charter Organization assigns the same Charter Organization Representative to all of the ward Scouting units

- Charter all Scout units in the ward annually.
- Register boys and adult leaders.
- See that Tour Plans are completed, signed, and submitted.
- Attend district committee meetings and the annual council business meeting.
- Attend Scout training as necessary.
- Encourage adults involved in Scouting to become properly trained soon after their call.
- Help organize a functioning Scouting committee.
- Conduct the annual Friends of Scouting (FOS) campaign.
- Help provide recognition for boys, young men, and their leaders.

The Primary Presidency's Responsibilities

"The ward Primary presidency, under the direction of a counselor in the bishopric, has responsibility for Scouting for eight-, nine-, ten-, and eleven-year-old boys. The Church does not participate in Scouting programs for boys younger than eight years old. A member of the presidency is responsible to see that Scouting is organized appropriately." (Scouting Handbook, page 3)

- Register with the Boy Scouts of America.
- Receive BSA training.
- Serve on the appropriate ward Scouting committee.
- Ensure that the Church policies are followed.
- Coordinate Scouting with the Faith in God program.
- Encourage leaders to attend Scout training.
- Help leaders understand how Scouting can strengthen families and accomplish the purpose of Primary.
- Help boys and adult complete registration forms.
- Attend activities to support and evaluate the quality of the program.
- Review each boy's progress and participation.
- Ensure boys attend day camp and, if necessary, help plan day camp.

Cubmaster / Scoutmaster
- Provide overall pack / troop leadership.
- Lead in planning the pack / troop meeting.
- Lead monthly pack meetings / scheduled troop meetings.
- Coordinate unit membership, recruiting, and transition.

Leadership Skills for the Cubmaster / Scoutmaster
- Working with the team.
- Effective communications.
- Understanding and working with boys.
- Project Scout spirit.

Words of Wisdom for Working with Cub Scouts
- Boys need a fast-moving program.
- Alternate energetic activities with quiet ones.
- Hands-on is better than lecture.
- Boys will learn self-control when given guidelines.
- Codes of Conduct work when used consistently.

Cub Scout / Webelos Den Leader
- Give leadership to den program planning.
- Plan, prepare, and run den meetings.
- Lead the den at pack events.
- Work with pack leaders to ensure den success.
- Participate in pack program planning.

EYOS Leader
Either the Primary teacher of eleven-year-old boys or another capable adult may serve as the group's Scout leader. This leader should:
- Work under the direction of a member of the Primary presidency, meeting regularly to discuss the Scouting program and each boy's progress.
- Register as the eleven-year-old Scout leader (assistant Scoutmaster) and attend the Boy Scout troop committee meetings.
- Attend Scout training as applicable.
- Attend other Primary meetings as invited.
- Encourage and help each boy achieve the Faith in God award and advance in Scouting.
- See that the boys participate in a day camp and help plan it if requested.

Pack / Troop Trainer's Responsibilities

- Conduct orientation for new families and unit leaders.
- Promote and track Position Specific Training (Online).
- Present training ideas and information at unit committee meetings.
- Conduct other training with assistance from the stake.
- Encourage unit leaders to attend ongoing training, such as roundtables, council or district training events, Wood Badge, etc.
- Track adult leader training and make recommendations.
- Remain current on BSA and Church Scouting policies and programs.

Unit Commissioner / Stake Young Men Presidency

The unit commissioner is a Boy Scout position not a Church calling. Districts assign unit commissioners to specific units to promote healthy Scouting units. *"The stake Young Men presidency, under the direction of the stake presidency, conducts training and coordinates support for the individual Aaronic Priesthood Scouting programs in each ward. They register as unit commissioners and serve as liaisons to Scouting units within the stake. They also participate in district committee meetings and roundtables. Members of the stake Young Men presidency should attend Scout training, as applicable."* (Scouting Handbook, page 2)

- Membership inventory (annually).
- Uniform inspection (pack in fall, Boy Scouts in fall and spring).
- Quality measurement (annually).
- Unit leadership inventory (ongoing).
- Charter presentation ceremony (thirty days after renewal).
- Youth Protection (promote training).
- Council/district two-way communication about upcoming training, activities, resources, and recognition.
- Ongoing support when requested.

Stake Primary Presidency

The stake Primary presidency, under the direction of the stake presidency, provides ongoing encouragement for ward Primaries by:

- Coordinate support for the Scouting programs in each ward.
- Provides instruction for ward Primary presidencies.
- Encourage ward Primary Scout leaders to participate in basic and other approved training.
- Help ward Primary presidencies understand Church Scouting policies and how the Scouting and Faith in God programs work together.
- Plan day camps, when needed.

Volunteer Leadership

Strength of the Boy Scout program is its volunteer leadership. Volunteer leaders and those who are called to serve in the ward and stake positions are an example of Scouting's principles of service to others. Parents are a logical source of leaders in the Scouting program and Scouting needs every parent's help to be a successful program. Parents volunteer not only to serve Scouting, but also to help their son and his friends, and to be a positive influence on the youth in the ward and community. Parents should register with the BSA as committee members.

Being a leader is fun, challenging, and rewarding. Leaders find that their experiences help them to become better parents. The following are some of the many dividends that will enrich their life as leaders dedicate time, talents, and enthusiasm to Scouting:

- Fun and fellowship with other families, sharing the pride in the boys' accomplishments.
- The privilege of helping to enrich and strengthen families.
- A chance to help boys learn good citizenship and to help shape them into men who have strength of character and are sensitive to the needs of others.
- The opportunity to help make a difference in the lives of boys, as they grow strong in mind and body.
- A code to live by which will set a worthwhile example for both boys and adults.
- The satisfaction of being a member of a worldwide movement, and pride in being publicly identified as a part of this organization.
- Wearing the Scouting uniform is a visible way of showing a belief in the ideals and objectives of the Boy Scouts.

Training Opportunities

This excerpt from the BSA's Annual Report reminds us that it takes a continuing training effort to prepare our youth to make ethical choices over their lifetime.

"It takes more than merit badges, handbooks, and uniforms for Boy Scout councils across America to have successful Cub Scout packs, Boy Scout troops, and Venturing crews. It's the people on the front line—council and district volunteers and unit-serving executives—who make the real difference in bringing the quality program of the Boy Scouts of America to the youth of our nation." The council and districts program calendar, local newsletter, and web sites will include details about time and location for training opportunities!

Scout Training

Training for Scout leaders is based on a stepping-stone approach. Each stone represents additional training and insight based on what was learned before.

Assuring that training programs are available keeps the council's professional and volunteer staffs busy. Cub Scouting succeeds because the council cares to make sure that leaders know how to organize and conduct quality programs. A leader's training begins when he or she is called. After accepting the calling, another leader or member of the committee begins the education process with the basics of where and when the unit meets.

"Young Men and Primary leaders who are called to Scouting responsibilities should receive training in Scouting principles, policies, and procedures as used by the Church. Trained Scout leaders who understand and live the gospel, understand priesthood governance, and understand the Scouting program are better able to serve young men and boys involved in Scouting activities." (Scouting Handbook, page 1)

Leaders working with boys and young men should complete the following BSA-required training:

- **Youth Protection** (Mandatory training available online, to be completed before service with youth begins).
- **Fast Start** (available online, to be completed within the first month of service).
- **This Is Scouting** (available online, to be completed during the first year of service).
- **Position-Specific Training for Cub Scouts, Boy Scouts, Varsity, and Venturing** (to be completed during the first year of service).
- **Introduction to Outdoor Leadership Skills** for Boy Scout, Varsity, and Venturing leaders (to be completed during the first year of service).

There is an interactive video available at www.lds.org under serving in the Primary which discusses the purpose of Cub Scouting and correlating Faith and God and Scouting. Other training is available at www.LDS-Scouting.org. It is very important to understand the LDS guidelines when participating in district and council training or reading the BSA materials. There are distinct differences in the methods not the aims of Scouting.

"Stake Young Men and Primary presidencies also offer ongoing training and support for ward Young Men, Primary, and Scouting leaders. In addition, the BSA provides monthly roundtables to help leaders learn Scouting methods and skills; it also offers a variety of optional training courses such as Wood Badge, The Trainer's EDGE, and others. Stake and ward budget allowance funds may be used for adult Scouting training. In cooperation with the Boy Scouts of America, the Church holds an optional Priesthood Leadership Conference on Scouting at the Philmont Scout Ranch in Cimarron, New Mexico. This weeklong course for stake presidency members emphasizes the priesthood basis for Scouting in Church units and teaches how Scouting can be used to reinforce priesthood purposes and gospel principles."

"Training courses that require overnight activities should not be attended by mixed groups of adult men and women unless both genders have appropriate sleeping and personal care arrangements that are not in immediate proximity to each other. Where possible, leaders should attend training offered on days other than Sunday." (Scouting Handbook, page 1)

Basic Training

All adult leaders working with Scouts of all ages are required to take **BSA Youth Protection** (YP) training prior to working with youth. Adult leader Youth Protection training is on-line or taught by BSA district or council trainers. Training can be provided on the unit level by a pack or troop trainer. Except for **Youth Protection**, all other training on www.MyScouting.org requires the leaders to register and set up an account. Every adult leader is assigned a unique number when they initially register with the BSA. The member number is found on the registration card or may be obtained from the unit recharter paperwork. If they do not have the number, please contact the council Scout office and request your registration number.

- **Fast Start Training** may come from a member of the unit or district training team. Its purpose is to get the program for the youth members up and running as quickly as possible. The Fast Start online presentation for Scout leaders located on www.MyScouting.org is designed to present the basic structure and concepts of Scouting to new leaders. This is best viewed before accepting a calling to work with boys or to serve on the pack committee. If there are going to be issues related to time commitment or conflicts, it is better to understand and address them prior to accepting the call. Fast Start training in Spanish and English is available for the Boy Scout program as well as Cub Scouts.

- **This is Scouting** is an online training session that is taken once. This course is an introductory session that highlights the values, aims, history, funding, and methods of Scouting. It addresses how these aims and methods are reached in an age-appropriate style within Cub Scouting, Boy Scouting, Varsity Scouting, and Venturing. Because this course is taken by all leaders (Cub Scouting to Venturing), each leader needs to complete this training only once, even if he or she later accepts a different leadership calling in the pack, troop, team, or crew.

- **Position Specific** provides details on how to get started in the new calling. It is also completed online and must be taken each time an individual is called to a new Scouting position. Leaders can take the training in any order. It is possible for new leaders to take **Position Specific** first to get started then take **This is Scouting**. Cub Scout Den Leaders/Assistant Den Leaders, Webelos Den Leaders/Assistant Webelos Den Leaders, Cubmasters/Assistant Cubmasters, and Pack Committee Members can complete this training easily in an evening then refer back to it when they have questions. These courses focus upon the specific role a leader has when working in Cub Scouting.

If the leader changes positions (for example from den leader to committee chair) the **Leader Specific Training** course for that new calling is required. The leader is considered fully trained upon completion of **Youth Protection**, **This is Scouting**, and **Position Specific** training for that position.

Supplemental training and continuing education take many forms. You may be an avid reader of *Scouting Magazine*. Or, you may be a faithful participant at your district roundtable or other special training events. Each provides continuing education to help leaders fulfill their calling and meet the needs of the youth they are responsible for.

Additional Training Opportunities

- **Roundtable** – Hosted monthly in each district, this meeting provides information updates and theme or merit badge based program ideas. This monthly district in-service meeting is designed to provide information of upcoming events and hands-on how-to training on many subjects. Rally training, and re-charter training are hosted at the district roundtables and offer information about completing that dreaded paperwork and other timely updates.

- **Outdoor Leader Skills** – For Scout leaders builds skills with the **Leave No Trace** emphasis on our Outdoor Code. **Okpik** – Cold Weather Camping – Expands your skills with the added challenge of dealing with Mother Nature. **BALOO** – Basic Adult Leader Outdoor Orientation – Is an introduction to camping for leaders in the Cub Scout. Note: LDS packs do not participate in over-night camping.

- **Council or District Training Day** (Including Cub Scout Pow Wow) – Timely and topical, hands-on workshops for all programs – as well as a series of basic classes available in this day long program. This is a one-day event, usually held on a Saturday, where Scout leaders take a variety of interesting and informative classes that help them provide a quality program.

- **Commissioner's Conference** and **Council Leadership Training** are available for members of the bishoprics and stake leadership.

- **University of Scouting (Lord Baden-Powell University)** – This is an annual event designed to provide a more academic approach in examining the various aspects of adult leadership in Scouting. This is a multi-council event which draws on the expertise of professional and volunteer Scouters.

- **Trainer's Edge** (previously **Trainer Development Conference**) – Presentation techniques for trainers and roundtable staff is also recommended for pack trainers.

- **Wood Badge** – To hone your leadership skills, there is advanced training called Wood Badge. This weeklong (or two three-day sessions) course is considered the premier training course for Scout leaders. Based on recognized leadership principles, the course prepares and enhances a leader's ability to provide the needed adult leadership in Scouting.

- Continuing education may extend beyond the local council's boundaries at one of the national training camps such as **Philmont** Scout Ranch in Cimarron, New Mexico or the **Seabase** in Florida.

- **Little Philmont** is designed to help stake and ward leaders in the Primary and Aaronic Priesthood understand the Scouting program as a valuable resource as they work with boys and young men to help them achieve Primary and Aaronic Priesthood objectives.

Sample Training Awards

Cub Scouter Award

Description: Gold over light blue knot on blue field with blue border.

Award Requirements:

Tenure:

- Complete two years as a registered adult leader in a Cub Scout pack.

Training:

- Complete Fast Start training, if available for your position.
- Complete This Is Scouting and specific training for any Cub Scouting position.
- Complete Youth Protection training.
- During each year of tenure for this award, participate in a Cub Scout leader Pow Wow or University of Scouting, or attend at least four roundtables.

Performance: Do any five of the following:

- Assist in planning a pack program that results in advancement in rank by a minimum of 50 percent of pack members each year.
- Serve as an adult leader related to a pack that earns the national Quality Unit Award.
- Serve as leader of a blue and gold dinner, pinewood derby, space derby, rain gutter regatta, field day, picnic or other Cub Scout pack activity.
- Give leadership to a promotional effort that results in at least 60 percent of pack families subscribing to Boys' Life magazine.
- Develop or update a Tiger Cub or Cub Scout den activity book listing local places to go, things to do, costs, distances, etc., for the five Tiger Cub areas, or for at least 12 Cub Scout themes.
- Give leadership to planning and conducting a pack service project.
- Organize participation of a pack in the Cub Scout Academics and Sports program.
- Help conduct two annual pack Friends of Scouting campaigns.
- Serve as a leader for members of your pack attending a Cub Scout day camp or resident camp.

LDS Guide to Scouting in the Primary

Scout Leader's Training Award

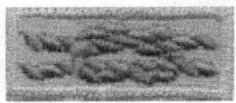

Description: green on green knot on tan field with tan border.

Award Requirements:

Tenure:

- Complete a total of 2 years as a registered adult Boy Scout leader.

Training:

- Complete Boy Scout Leader Fast Start training.
- Complete New Leader Essentials.
- Complete Scoutmaster Basic Leader Training.
- Complete Introduction to Outdoor Leader Skills.
- Complete Youth Protection Training.

Performance: Do any five of the following:

- Participate in a support role for five overnight campouts.
- Help with two annual unit and/or district Friends of Scouting presentations.
- Participate actively in three troop parents' nights or courts of honor.
- Help organize or reorganize a Boy Scout troop.
- Help supervise or support a troop money-earning project.
- Participate in a supplemental training course at either the council or national level.
- Serve on the staff of a council or district training event.
- Serve as a merit badge counselor for at least five Scouts.
- Successfully complete Wood Badge training.
- Fulfill requirements of a troop committee function from the Troop Committee Guidebook.
- Assist actively with a Webelos den for 6 months.
- Participate in six Boy Scout leader roundtables.

Funding

Funding

The Scouting Handbook references the Church Handbook 2 in discussing Scout funding. *"Ward budgets should be used to purchase Scouting badges, awards, and materials, as determined by local leaders."* (Scouting Handbook, page 6) The fees paid by the stake include registration and rechartering fees. *"Stakes register all boys and young men ages 8 through 15. Young men ages 16 and 17 should be registered when they are pursuing rank advancements or when the ward sponsors a Venturing Crew. Scout leaders should also be registered. Registration fees for youth and adults are paid by the stakes and reimbursed from general Church funds. Registration forms and fees for youth and adults should be submitted to the local council in conjunction with the annual re-chartering and on an on-going basis as young men advance to Boy Scouts, Varsity Scouts, or Venturing."* (Scouting Handbook, page 5)

Additional fees for accident and health insurance coverage during chartering are not paid to local councils.

The cost of *Boys' Life* magazine is covered by the family or in some cases by the ward. It is cheaper to order the magazine during rechartering or when an application is submitted than to order it directly from *Boy's Life*.

The cost of a new uniform is listed on www.scoutstuff.org. A Scout handbook is approximately $10 and a Cub Scout shirt and hat is about $50. The cost of the Boy Scout shirt, pants, and sash is about $100. In addition to purchasing the uniforms online, they can be purchased at the Scout shops located at local councils, at area merchants who sell BSA uniforms, or clothing resale shops. Many units (ward and stake) have uniform exchange programs.

The primary source of funding for the Scouting program and activities is the ward budget. Fund raising projects are approved for purchasing capital equipment and to pay for Boy Scout long-term camp or Cub Scout day camp. The ward pays for activities and awards, and parents pay for the uniforms and Boy's Life.

Wards determine the cost of the program, starting with a form similar to the one below. First calculate the annual cost then submit it to the ward Primary for budgeting purposes. The chart below reflects a Cub Scout pack of six boys with a total budget of $734.

Boy Costs			Leader Costs		
Boys' Life (6)	$12.00	$72.00	Leader's Training	$25.00	$75.00
Advancement Awards (6)	$20.00	$120.00	Leader's Books	$20.00	$60.00
Den Meetings (22)	$3.00	$66.00	Gas – Field Trips	$10.00	$30.00
Monthly Pack Meetings (10)	$3.00	$30.00	Leader's Uniform	$97.30	$0.00
Cub Scouts Day Camp Cost varies, paid by parents	$130.00	$0.00	District Dinner Paid by leader	$25.00	$0.00
Pinewood Derby (6)	$8.00	$48.00			
Blue and Gold Banquet (6)	$10.00	$60.00			
Handbooks (6)	$8.00	$48.00			
Uniform, paid by parents	$35.00	$0.00			
Supplies / Equipment	$125.00	$125.00			
Subtotal - Boys		$569.00	Subtotal - Leaders		$165.00
Total Pack Budget					$734.00

Boys should not feel excluded from participating in the program because they cannot afford to pay for activities. On the other hand, den leaders should not pay for den meeting supplies. Leader training can come out of the ward budget.

A stake or ward uniform exchange will keep the costs at a reasonable level as will a ward resource library where leadership books, merit badge books, and equipment are shared. A committee member or parent can be assigned to maintain resources.

Friends of Scouting

With the changes in funding for the Boy Scouts of America, it is important for units to support the local council through donations to Friends of Scouting. To maintain quality Scouting programs, the council requires financial support from all units to provide activities including Cub Scout day camp and Boy Scout camp.

"The Church supports the annual Friends of Scouting drive. These funds provide financial support for the local BSA council. Stake presidents and bishops oversee the drive in their units." (Scouting Handbook, page 6)

Church Policies on Scouting and Funding

Details on the church policies on funding can be obtained from the Handbook 2: Administering the Church (November 2010).

Scouting

Where Scouting is authorized by the Church, Scouting is the Activity Day program for boys eight – ten and Boy Scouts for eleven year old boys.

All adult Scout leaders register and receive Youth Protection training before they meet with the boys. *"In the United States, registered adult leaders receive liability protection from the Boy Scouts of America."*

The Church pays for registering young men and adult leaders in Scouting for unit chartering from the stake general checking account. The Church provides these funds in addition to the budget allowance.

Funding for Activities

Funding for Scouting activities, where they are authorized by the Church, should come from the ward budget.

Funding for an Annual Camp or Similar Activity

Annual camp is paid from ward funds if sufficient. If not, participants pay for part or all of it. If funds from participants are not sufficient, the bishop may authorize one group fund-raising activity annually. In no case should the cost prohibit anyone from participating nor should the cost be excessive.

Funding for Equipment and Supplies

The bishop may authorize one fund raiser to purchase equipment and supplies when the ward budget is not sufficient to cover the cost of the materials. Church property may not be used by individuals or families. Church funds may not be used to purchase uniforms for individuals.

Funding for Activities

It is important that activities have little or no cost. All expenses must be approved by the bishop or stake president before they are incurred. All activities, programs, and supplies should be paid for from the stake or ward funds. Members should not pay fees to participate or for materials, supplies, rental or admission fees. Long-distance transportation should not be at their expense. Members can provide food for activities if it does not put an undue burden on them.

A fund raiser may be approved if the ward does not have sufficient funds to cover day camp for Primary-age boys. In no case should the expenses for an annual camp be excessive or prohibit a member from participating.

Fund-Raising Activities

If a fund-raising activity is approved, it should provide a meaningful value or service that provides a positive experience and builds unity.

- Contributions must be voluntary and no one should feel obligated to contribute.
- Fund-raising activities should not advertise beyond the ward's boundaries.
- Products or services are not sold door-to-door.
- Activities must not be taxable.
- Activities should not be completed with paid labor, either by employees or by contract.
- Do not hire entertainment or pay performers when admission is charged to raise money.
- Do not sell commercial goods or services, including food storage items.
- No raffles, lotteries, or bingo.

The Friends of Scouting fund drive in the United States will continue as a separate, voluntary solicitation.

Each stake and ward needs to prayerfully determine how a quality program will be funded in the units. Challenges will exist and can be overcome as the unit leaders work together to plan and prepare for the needs of the boys and young men.

Cub Scout Program

Cub Scout Den

A boy is a member of a den of four-to-eight boys which:

1. Meets regularly at the chapel, in a home, or in an outdoor setting.
2. Includes games, crafts, skits, songs, ceremonies, and field trips.
3. Is led by a den leader called by the bishopric.
4. Is assisted by an assistant den leader (parents may rotate assisting), a Den Chief (an older Boy Scout), and a Denner (a Cub Scout).
5. Boy and leaders wear uniforms.

Cub Scout Den Meetings

- Before the meeting
- Gathering
- Opening prayer
- Business items
- Activities
- Closing prayer
- After the meeting

Den Meeting Structure

It is imperative that each den meeting be carefully planned by the den leaders. The following explains the normal parts of a den meeting:

- **Before the meeting** – Den and Webelos leaders, their assistants, and den chiefs arrive a few minutes before the den meeting to set up and review together the activities planned for the den meeting.

- **Gathering** – As the boys are slowly arriving, an activity is planned to hold the boy's interest until all of the boys arrive.

- **Opening / Prayer** – The recitation of the Scout Promise, Prayer, Pledge of Allegiance and any special announcements begin the meeting.

- **Business Items** – Quick announcements are appropriate, written announcements are a better method of communicating with parents. Newsletters can be in a paper format or electronically emailed. Advancement records can be maintained online with parents taking responsibility for entering achievements and electives.

- **Lesson/Activities/Activity Badges** – Advancement activities for Wolf, Bear, and Webelos are accomplished. These are outlined later in this guide.

- **Snack (optional)** – It is nice on occasion to have a refreshing snack for the boys as the meeting nears its end.

- **Closing / Prayer** – Review what the boys need to do to get ready for the next den meeting. It could be a quick discussion about behavior problems, a time to give the boys messages that they need to take to their parents, and a final check that each boy has his book to take home. This time should also include a closing prayer.

Den Code of Conduct

A least once a year, boys in the pack discuss what a den meeting will be like and what will be accomplished at the Cub Scout meetings and activities. Review the Cub Scout sign and let the Scouts know that the sign is used to get the boys attention. The boys are asked to set rules which maybe harder than the rules adults would set. The rules are written down on poster board and displayed at each den meeting. Here is a sample den Code of Conduct:

- I will wait my turn to speak.
- I will always speak respectfully.
- I will keep my hands, feet, and personal items to myself.
- I will listen to Akela.
- I will keep my tongue in my mouth.
- I will talk nicely to other people.
- I will remember that in the Church, I will walk slowly and talk softly.

Rewarding Good Behavior (coup and beads)

When a boy is good and actively participates, it is important to reward the good behavior. One method is the Indian coup and beads. The boys make a coup with either leather or vinyl strings so it can be worn on the belt with his belt loops. When a boy does something good color-coded beads are added to the coup.

- Blue Bead: Coming in full uniform to the meeting including the neckerchief.
- Red bead: Advancing one rank.
- Orange Bead: Attending pack meeting and bringing something to display.
- Green Bead: Participating in conservation or service project.
- Purple Bead: Participate in district or council event.
- Yellow bead: Not receiving a "strike" at the meeting (three warnings to follow code of conduct).

Den Chief

Den leaders may ask for the assistance of an older Boy Scout who can serve as the Den Chief. The den chief assists in teaching lessons, leading and teaching games, skills, songs and skits, setting up and cleaning up, and helping the den leader in working with boys who need additional attention. Some guidelines for using a den chief include:

- Request their time for a specific length of time (i.e. six months).
- Get their commitment and their parent's support.
- Request that they check their calendar and give you dates they cannot attend.
- Plan in advance how you will utilize the den chief.

When the Cub Scouts meet at the same time as the Young Men / Boy Scout troop, it may be difficult to utilize a den chief from the same ward's Boy Scout troop. However, during the summer, a den chief can be extremely helpful at day camp. In addition to assisting the Cub Scouts, they serve as an example that the boys will follow.

Denner

The Cub Scout Denner and Assistant Denner are Cub Scouts who rotate the responsibility to lead the meeting and have specific responsibilities which may include:

- Help set up the facility.
- Lead the flag and other ceremonies.
- Organize games and songs.
- Assume other leadership duties.

Pack 174 Responsibility Chart

	Denner	Asst Denner	Msuic	Closing Prayer	Snack
8/24	Gallagher	Brigham	Anthony	Nicholas	
9/1	Gallagher	Brigham	Atticus	Anthony	
9/14	Gallagher	Brigham	Nicholas	Atticus	Anthony
9/28	Gallagher	Brigham	Anthony	Nicholas	Atticus
10/6	Brigham	Anthony	Gallagher	Atticus	Nicholas
10/12	Brigham	Anthony	Nicholas	Gallagher	Atticus
10/26	Brigham	Anthony	Atticus	Nicholas	Gallagher
11/3	Anthony	Nicholas	Gallagher	Atticus	Brigham
11/9	Anthony	Nicholas	Brigham	Gallagher	Atticus
11/23	Anthony	Nicholas	Atticus	Brigham	Dallin
12/1	Nicholas	Atticus	Dallin	Anthony	Brigham
12/14	Nicholas	Atticus	Brigham	Dallin	Anthony

The Denner wears two yellow cords and the Assistant Denner wears one yellow cord on their left epaulet to show their position in the den. The rotation is assigned by the den leader to ensure that everyone is given the opportunities to learn how to lead. Nine-year-olds are assigned to be a Denner to complete Bear Achievement 24.

Cub Scout Pack

Boys are members of the ward's pack which:
1. Is made up of one or more dens.
2. Meet once a month at a pack meeting with all Cub Scout families invited.
    a. Includes games, skits, songs, ceremonies, and presentation of badges that the boys earned that month.
    b. Is led by the Cubmaster who is called by the bishopric.
    c. Is the climax of the month's den meetings and activities.
    d. Provides recognition for Cub Scouts.
    e. Involves all family members.
    f. Introduces the new theme or value for the month.

Cub Scout Pack Meetings

- Before the meeting
- Gathering
- Flag ceremony
- Opening song
- Opening prayer
- Cub Scout Promise and Law
- Opening ceremony – Introduction of the Value (theme)
- Awards and recognition
- Program / activity
- Cub Scout den skits and stunts, Webelos demonstration, games
- Closing song
- Closing prayer
- After the meeting

Pack Meeting Structure

Once a month, the Cub Scout pack meeting is held to display the boy's exhibits, make presentations, present individual awards and advancements, and introduce the value or theme for the next month.

- **Set-up** – Parents and boys who are assigned to set up should arrive at the meeting place before the meeting time and set up chairs and display tables as required.

- **Gathering Activity** – The den assigned to organize the gathering activity is responsible for providing a fun activity to keep the boys busy until all of the Cub Scouts arrive.

- **Opening Ceremony / Prayer / Song** – Boys are assigned to say the opening prayer, lead the music, participate in the flag ceremony, lead the pledge-of-allegiance, lead the recitation of the Scout Promise and Law, and conduct the meeting.

- **Awards and Advancements** – The Cubmaster presents the boys with the advancement/award. When the Wolf, Bear, or Webelos award is given, there is a pin that the boy pins on the parents' shirt lapel or on a ribbon with other recognition pins.

- **Program / Activity** – A theme or value related program may be scheduled.

- **Games / Skits / Songs** – Dens are assigned a part of the program, which should relate to the theme or value, be positive, uplifting, build confidence and self-esteem, and should not include any "bathroom" humor or make fun of any group of people.

- **Closing Ceremony** – Colors are retired and a Cub Scout says a closing prayer.

- **Snack (Optional)** – Occasionally a snack may be appropriate.

LDS Guide to Scouting in the Primary

Flag Ceremony

It is important for the den leader to know that during the pledge of allegiance the boys who are in uniform are to salute the flag with the Cub Scout salute, while the boys out-of-uniform are to place their hand over their heart. This is the same for the den leaders. Caps and hats that are NOT part of the Cub Scout uniform are to be removed before the pledge of allegiance.

The U.S. Flag

When displaying the flag in a manner other than on poles and in flag stands it is important to know the proper way to display it. The following shows how a flag should be hung when placed on a wall or hung from a rope.

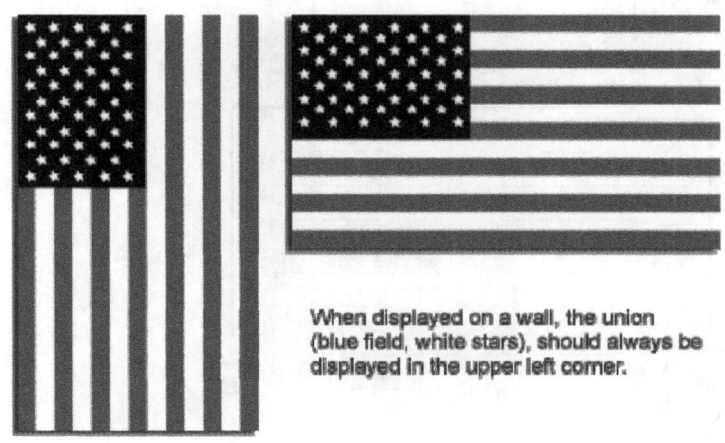

When displayed on a wall, the union (blue field, white stars), should always be displayed in the upper left corner.

Folding the Flag

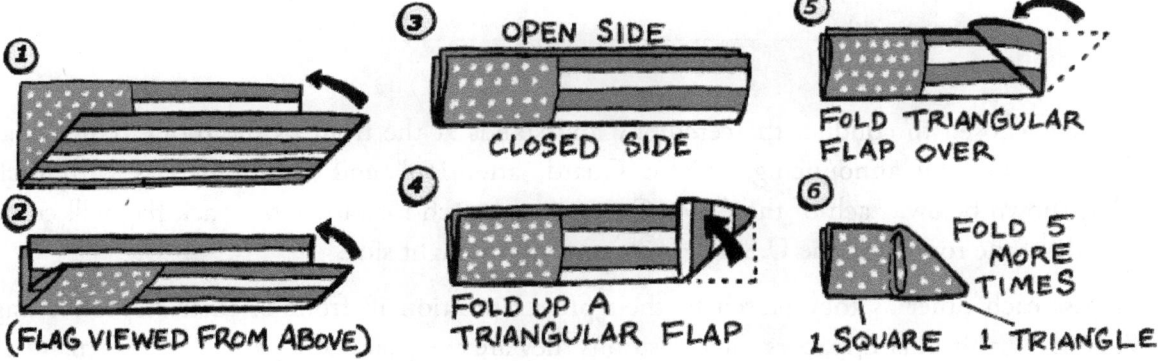

The following is what is said and done by the Cub Scouts during the "presentation of colors" (opening flag ceremony) and the "retrieval of colors" (closing flag ceremony).

Flag Opening Ceremony

Prior to the pack meeting the Cub Scouts need to put flag stands in place at the front of the room. *Looking to the front*, the U.S. flag stand should be placed on the *left* and pack flag stand (if you have one) is placed on the right. Also prior to the meeting, the Cub Scouts that will be part of the color Guard(s) are chosen (2-4 for each Color Guard). The U.S. Flag Color Guard lines up in single file at the back of the room on the right. The pack flag color guard does the same only they are positioned at the back on the left. (See example shown below).

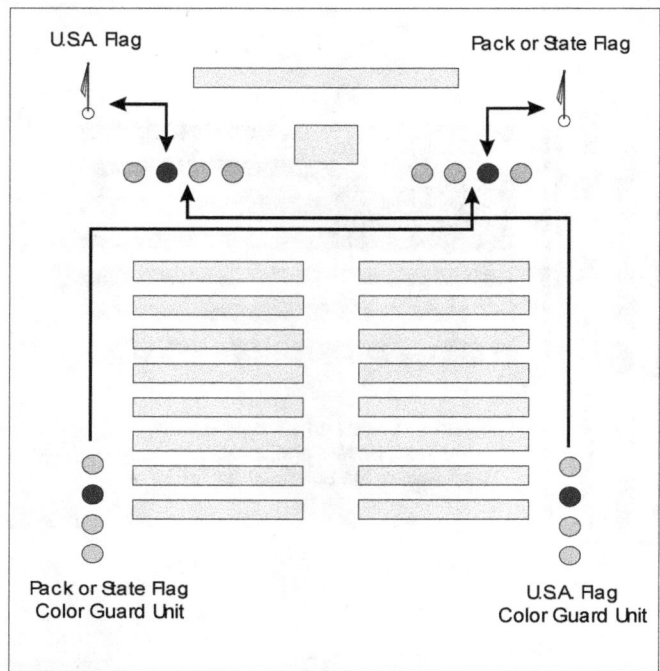

A Cub Scout is chosen to conduct the ceremony and stands at the front of the room. This Scout begins the ceremony by announcing, "Color Guard, attention" and then proceeds with each command as shown below. Each of the Color Guard lines march forward – the pack flag will come up the left side of the room and the U.S. flag will come up the right side.

They will pass each other as they march to their proper position in front of their respective flag stand. When the Color Guard reaches their positions they are commanded to halt. The command to "Post Colors" is given and the boy holding the U.S. flag places it in the stand first and then the boy holding the pack flag places it in the stand second. They then both return to their respective color guard unit. They then turn and face the flag and salute. The audience is asked to repeat the pledge of allegiance. After the pledge of allegiance the salute ends with the command of "Two" and the Color Guard is then dismissed.

Flag Opening Ceremony

- "Color Guard, attention."
- "Will the audience please rise." (Only if they are seated.)
- "Color Guard, present colors."
- "Salute."
- "Color Guard, halt!"
- "Color Guard, post colors."
- "Please repeat the pledge of allegiance." (Audience joins in the pledge of allegiance.)
- "Two" (means that the salute can end)
- "Color Guard, dismissed."
- "The audience will please be seated." (Only if the audience is seated.)

Flag Closing Ceremony (Retrieval)

The closing ceremony is done in like manner – the boys start in the rear of the room and march forward on command and then are halted. On command, they salute the flag. The salute ends with the command "Two." Then a single boy retrieves the U.S. flag first and then falls back into line with the other boys. The pack flag is then retrieved and that boy falls back in line. The Color Guard with the U.S. flag then marches off followed by the pack flag Color Guard.

- "Will the audience please rise." (Only if the audience is seated.)
- "Color Guard, advance."
- "Color Guard, salute."
- "Two."
- "Color Guard, retrieve colors." (Fold flag.)
- "The audience will please be seated." (Only if audience is seated.)

Pack and Den Flags

The following are examples of official pack and den flags

Pack and den flags can add some additional interest to the pack activities and pack meetings. They are also a source of pride when taken to Cub Scout district events. The official flags can be purchased from the BSA store or can be created by the den or pack.

Outdoor Flag Ceremony

Cub Scouts learn how to raise the flag outdoors as well as indoors.

Present the Colors and Retrieval: When the flag is raised in the morning, it is spoken of as "Colors." When the flag is lowered at the end of the day it is called "Retrieve."

Formation: The group proceeds in single file and forms a horseshoe around the flagpole and stands at attention. Color Guard (bearer and guards) then advance with the Color Bearer preceding the guards, who follow immediately behind in twos. They take position in front of the flagpole and stand at attention facing the pole during the entire ceremony.

Silence: There is absolute silence from the time the group moves forward until it returns to the starting point. The Color Guard is the "Official Guardian" of the flag and does not sing or speak.

Ceremony: The ceremony takes place after the flag has been raised or before it is lowered. The ceremony itself varies but often consists of the Pledge of Allegiance, the Promise and Law, patriotic or nature poetry, and songs.

Salute: The group gives full salute at Colors from the moment the flag starts upward holding salute until it reaches the top. At retrieve the Colors, the full salute begins the moment the flag starts down. The flag is lowered slowly, and the salute is held until it arrives at the bottom and is in the hands of the Color Guard.

Raising / Lowering: The clasps on the rope should be the same distance apart as the eyelets in the flag. All clasps should be fastened on the flag before it is started upward. At Colors, one guard may hold the flag as the Color Bearer attaches it to the rope before raising it briskly to the top. At Retrieval, the first two Color Guards may step forward to catch the flag as it is lowered so that is does not touch the ground. The upper corner of the flag should be in the Color Bearer's hands before he unfastens the clasps.

Folding: The flag is held by the Color Guard with the blue field nearest the flagpole. It is folded lengthwise in half, then again lengthwise in half, folding the blue field underneath toward the outside. The last couple (farthest away from the pole) begin folding the flag in a triangle. They fold until they can pass it on to other members of the Color Guard. This continues until the flag is in a triangle.

Placing Folded Flag: The Color Guard resumes its original position. One member of the first couple steps up in front of the Color Bearer with the folded flag. He places it in the bearer's outstretched hands, so that it can be carried point forward, then returns to position.

Return: After the ceremony the Color Guard returns to their original position.

Opening Commands:

Audience, attention.

Color Guard, attention.

Color Guard, advance.

Color Guard, present the Colors.

Audience, please join us in the Pledge Allegiance.

Color Guard, dismissed.

(Color Guard steps back one step and salutes the flag before retreating.)

Audience, dismissed.

(Prayer followed by Scout Promise, poem or song)

Retreat Commands:

Audience, attention.

Color Guard, advance.

(Thought / Poem / Play "Taps")

Color Guard, retrieve the Colors.

(Color guards salute the flag and step forward)

(Flag is lowered and folded)

Color Guard, dismissed.

Audience, dismissed.

Flag Retirement Ceremony

When the U.S. Flag becomes tattered or worn, it should be disposed of by burning.

1. Salute the flag and say the Pledge of Allegiance.

    I pledge allegiance to the Flag of the United States of America, and to the Republic for which it stands: one Nation under God, indivisible, With Liberty and Justice for all.

2. Lower the flag from the pole (or remove it from the staff) and carry it to the fire site.

3. Place the stars (as the audience sees them) in the upper left hand corner. This is an appropriate reading to start the ceremony:

    "Remember as you look at the Flag, it is the symbol of our nation, it is red because of human sacrifice; blue because of the true blue loyalty of its defenders; and white symbolizes liberty – our land of the free. The stars are symbols of the united efforts and hope in the hearts of the many people striving to keep America great."

4. Cut the field of blue from the stripes – have someone hold onto this piece.

5. Next, cut each stripe from the "whole" and lay each piece, one at a time, across the flames.

    These are some readings for each stripe:

    FIRST STRIPE: The 13 stripes stand for the thirteen original colonies which are; Massachusetts, Virginia, Pennsylvania, New York, Connecticut, Rhode Island, New Hampshire, Delaware, Maryland, North Carolina, South Carolina, Georgia, and New Jersey.

    SECOND STRIPE: The white stands for purity.

    THIRD STRIPE: The red stands for courage.

    FOURTH STRIPE: "Give me liberty or give me death".

    FIFTH STRIPE: "One if by land, two if the sea".

SIXTH STRIPE: We the people of the United States, in order to form a more perfect union, establish justice, ensure domestic tranquility, provide for the common defense, promote the general welfare, and secure the blessings of liberty to ourselves and our posterity, do ordain and establish this Constitution of the United States of America.

SEVENTH STRIPE: We hold these truths to be self evident that all men are created equal. They are endowed by their creator with certain inalienable rights. Among these are life, liberty, and the pursuit of happiness.

EIGHTH STRIPE: Congress shall make no law respecting an establishment of religion or prohibiting the free exercise thereof.

NINTH STRIPE: Congress shall make no law abridging the freedom of speech or press.

TENTH STRIPE: "Four score and seven years ago, our fathers brought forth to this continent a new nation, conceived in liberty and dedicated to the proposition that all men are created equal."

ELEVENTH STRIPE: The right of citizens of the United States to vote shall not be denied or abridged by the United States or by any state on account of sex.

TWELFTH STRIPE: "Ask not what your country can do for you, but what you can do for your country."

THIRTEENTH STRIPE: "One small step for man, one giant leap for mankind."

6. Group says together:

Pledge of Allegiance
I Pledge Allegiance to the flag of the United States of America and to the Republic for which it stands, one Nation under God, indivisible, with liberty and justice for all.

America

My country, 'tis of Thee,
Sweet Land of Liberty
Of thee I sing;
Land where my fathers died,
Land of the pilgrims' pride,
From every mountain side
Let Freedom ring.

Our fathers' God to Thee,
Author of Liberty,
To thee we sing,
Long may our land be bright
With Freedom's holy light,
Protect us by thy might
Great God, our King.

Nothing should ever be added to the ceremonial fire after the flag has been burned (out of respect). The next morning the boys that actually burned the flag and their leader will gather the ashes. This could be included as the last step of the ceremony if all of those in attendance choose to participate. The grommets are given as special recognition.

Cub Scout Activities

Day Camp

An activity that includes: crafts, games, nature, sports, BB-guns, archery, songs, and skits. Day camp sessions may run up to five days depending on the location, theme, and activities planning by the stake, district, or council.

No Cub Scout or Webelos overnight camping is permitted and no hiking on Sunday.

Pinewood Derby
Parents and sons, even entire wards, build race cars made from a block of wood then race their cars at the pinewood derby.

Rain Gutter Regatta
The boys form a block of wood into a boat, decorate it, and race it in a water-filled rain gutter with the boys blowing air through a straw into the sail of the boat.

Space Derby
Boys are provided kits to build a rubber-band powered rocket. The boys race their rockets by hanging them from a wire and letting the twisted propeller propel the rocket forward.

Bike Rodeo
The Cub Scout bike rodeo is an opportunity for the Cub Scouts to learn about bicycling safety and the thrill of bike riding. They navigate their way through a series of challenges that demonstrate their level of ability. The boys and their families learn about bike safety, maintenance, and repair.

Cubmobile
Stake, district, or council may have go-cart races called cubmobile. Instructions on building the cart and rules for racing should be followed to ensure the boy's safety.

Blue and Gold / Scouting Banquet
The Boy Scout birthday is celebrated annually in an activity usually held in February. All Scouting units in the ward can hold a Scouting banquet or the pack can plan a Blue and Gold banquet that recognizes Cub Scouts and their leaders. The ward does not observe a Scout Sunday or wear their Scout uniform during Sacrament meeting.

Service Projects and Other Activities
In addition to regular pack meetings and activities, the pack sponsors special projects and events throughout the year. These include Church and community service projects (Scouting for Food, Eagle service projects, conservation projects, etc.) and outdoor activities (rocket launch, picnics, campfires, swimming, hiking, forest preserve outings, outdoor flag ceremonies, etc.)

Outdoor Awards

World Conservation Badge – The temporary patch consists of a giant panda on violet Scout trefoil, violet trim with gold background. This award can be earned only once by a Cub Scout.

Cub Scout Outdoor Activity Award – Wolf, Bear, and Webelos have the opportunity to earn the Cub Scout Outdoor Activity Award. Boys may earn the award in each year as long as the requirements are completed each year. The first year, the boy will receive the pocket flap award, each successive time the award is earned; a wolf track pin may be added to the flap.

National Summertime Award – During the months of June, July, and August Cub Scouts and their families can participate in Scouting activities that are educational and fun! Participating in these summertime activities gives the Cub Scout, his den, and the pack an opportunity to earn the National Summertime Pack Award. Each boy who attends three activities earns a pin to wear on the Cub Scout Outdoor Activity Patch.

Boys' Life Magazine

A magazine for boys and adults, *Boys' Life* has interesting features on Scouting, sports, hobbies, magic, science, U.S. history, jokes, comics, and short stories. The nominal cost of the magazine is the responsibility of the parents or ward; it is an excellent magazine and worth the cost. Stories about boys and adults from the Church are frequently included.

Scouting Magazine

The BSA magazine for adult leaders includes information to support adults who provide a quality Cub Scout program. It includes updates on programs and what's new in Scouting. Changes in the program, new merit badges, changes in advancement requirements, best practices, and instructions on how to do many Scout crafts are regularly included in the magazine. All registered adults receive the Scouting Magazine because it is included in the adult registration fee.

The magazines are also online:
Boy's Life – www.boyslife.org
Scouting Magazine – www.scoutingmagazine.org

Especially for Cub Scout Parents

Orientation

When a family joins the pack the Primary presidency ensures that the parents receive very basic information about the Cub Scout program, so they know how to get started. This can occur individually or as a group. Documents posted on www.LDS-Scouting.org are available to provide parents with the information they need to begin their Scouting journey. Orientation packets include:

- An overview of each rank including the Bobcat badge requirements.
- Family Talent Survey Sheets for each parent to complete and return to the pack committee.
- Parents' Orientation Guide to LDS Scouting (copied from the web site.)
- A pack newsletter and annual calendar.
- Uniform inspection sheets.
- BSA applications for both the boy and his parents.

BSA Family Award

The BSA Family Award is an optional program that parents may want to take advantage of in addition to the activities planned by the pack for the Cub Scouts. The sample monthly plans in this guide and posted on the web site include activities from the BSA Family Award that correlate with the monthly core values. The experiences family members share as they complete the requirements for the family award will enrich family living and strengthen family relationships. The family will complete, within a 12-month period, five requirements to earn the award. Two of the requirements are mandatory and three may be the family's choice. The areas of focus are:

1. Learning through Fun and Adventure
2. Strengthening Family Relationships
3. Developing Character
4. Teaching Responsibility
5. Handling Difficult Situations

Families who are registered in Cub Scouting for several years may earn the award more than once. Each time the award is earned, the family will receive a BSA Family Award certificate.

The BSA Family Activity Book is the primary resource for the program. It is filled with suggested activities to enhance the children's personal development and enrich and strengthen the family. These activities could include going on field trips; telling stories; doing arts and crafts projects; playing games; participating in family discussions; or making lists, charts and scrapbooks. Included with most topics are recommended books for adults and children to read together.

Material on the program can be purchased online at www.scoutstuff.org or at a council scout shop.

LDS Program Planning

Many Cub Scout packs outside the LDS Church plan their program based on the school year with Cub Scouts moving from one rank to another based on the grade they are in. While it is true many units advance together and graduate in February into Boy Scouts together, LDS boys advance to the next rank on their birthday. Cross over ceremonies occur throughout the year and happen when the boy turns eleven and joins the eleven-year-old Scout patrol.

Fortunately, materials provided at roundtables coincide with the core values of Cub Scouting: January – Positive Attitude, February – Resourcefulness, March – Compassion, April – Faith, May – Health and Fitness, June – Perseverance, July – Courage, August – Honesty, September – Cooperation, October – Responsibility, November – Citizenship, December – Respect.

The LDS program defined in this guide utilizes achievements and activities that focus on the core values that are assigned to each month. Similar Wolf, Bear, and Webelos requirements are grouped together by months. Because many of the LDS packs are small, typically all of the Cub Scouts meet together to work on rank requirements.

The Boy Scouts of America publishes resources for leaders to help them prepare for their meetings. The *New Cub Scout Den and Pack Meeting Resource Guide* and the *Cub Scout Leader Book* contain information that is helpful if you first have a good understanding of the LDS guidelines. The *Scouting Handbook for Church Units* can be downloaded from www.lds.org to provide answers to many questions on the Scouting program in the Church of Jesus Christ of Latter-day Saints. The *Academic and Sports Program Guide* plus song, activity, ceremony, and other publications provide useful information that is used to plan meaningful Cub Scout meetings and activities. The best resource is the Cub Scout handbooks: Wolf, Bear, and Webelos. The Webelos Leader's Guide is also a tool for Webelos leaders and includes guidelines specifically for LDS Scouting.

Annual Pack Program Planning

Usually in August or September, the pack leaders, parents, committee members, ward volunteers, Primary presidency, and teachers meet to plan the year. After the meeting, dates can be submitted to the ward to be placed on the ward calendar for the following year. A successful year is dependent on having important resources available when and where they are needed.

District and council dates for training and events are normally published in the spring for the following year. With these dates in hand, the pack can plan for the coming year by making assignments, planning activities, and involving all parents. The meeting can be held in conjunction with a pack meeting and is chaired by the committee chairman.

Pack Monthly Planners

Felicia Brandt, the Northeast Illinois Council Training Chairman, described the LDS Cub Scout program as a one-room school house. It is an exceptional methodology that works!

The documents in this section can be downloaded from www.LDS-Scouting.org and copies can be made for ward use. The example of an annual plan on pages 72 – 74 in this guide is available as an Excel spreadsheet that can be updated and printed. It includes macros to simplify the planning process. The "Twelve Month" and "Nine Month" examples provide a starting point in preparing an annual plan. The keys to adapting the Cub Scout delivery method to LDS units include:

- Involving the boy's family through effective communication and providing clear directions on what can be done at home.
- Tracking the boy's progress and adapting the program to meet their needs.
- Identifying alternatives to the outlined program when the boys have already completed the suggested activities.
- Utilizing the Cub Scout Sports and Academic belt loops and pins to augment the boy's activities in den and pack meetings. For example: the boys will be in the Cub Scout program for three years so the pack can rotate between soccer, kickball, and flag football and cover each once every three years. Also the boys can complete the requirements but another form of recognition can be used in place of the belt loops.

In this section the matrix for each rank provides an overview of the rotation so each boy has the opportunity to advance within the first six months of his birthday. Using the meeting plan outlined in the *Cub Scout Den and Pack Meeting Resource Guide* benefits boys whose birthdays fall around the beginning of the school year. Using a flexible calendar and planning the year based on the needs of the boys, LDS units provide an exceptional Scouting experience for Cub Scouts and Boy Scouts with an excellent record of advancement and retention.

It is important to understand each boy's needs and develop a program that augments what he does at home and ensures that he is recognized for his accomplishments.

It is key to KIS-MIF …. "KEEP IT SIMPLE – MAKE IT FUN"

Note: **Fun for the Family** in the last row of each month's matrix refers to the BSA Family Award. See page 65 for more information on this optional program.

Wolf Matrix

Achievements are repeated to ensure Cub Scouts earn their Wolf badge in six months.

Month	Achievement	Electives
January	Cooking and Eating (A8)	Spare Time (E5) Be an Artist (E12)
February	Start a Collection (A6) Your Living World (A7)	Tie It Right (E17)
March	Keep Your Body Healthy (A3) Making Choices (A12)	Computers (E21) Say it Right (E22)
April	Know Your Home and Community (A4) Be Safe at Home and On the Street (A9) Duty to God (A11)	Spare Time Fun – Kites (E5) Machine Power (E8)
May	Feats of Skill (A1) Tools for Fixing and Building (A5) Be Safe at Home and On the Street (A9) Cooking and Eating (A8)	Sports (E20)
June	Swimming (A1) Family Fun (A10)	Grow Something (E15) Fishing (E19) Sports (E20) Let's Go Camping (E23)
July	Your Flag (A2)	Play a Game (E4) Sing-Along (E11) Outdoor Adventure (E18)
August	Start a Collection (A6) Your Living World (A7)	Birds (S13) Grow Something (E15)
September	Feats of Skill (A1) Keep Your Body Healthy (A3)	Books, Books, Books (E6) Foot Power (E7) Sports (E20)
October	Know Your Home and Community (A4) Be Safe at Home and On the Street (A9) Making Choices (A12)	Family Alert (E16)
November	Your Flag (A2) Your Living World (A7) Duty to God (A11)	American Indian Signs (E1) American Indian Lore (E10)
December	Family Fun (A10) Tools for Fixing and Building (A5)	Be an Actor (E2) Make It Yourself (E3) Pets (E14)

Note: Play a Game (E4), Sing-Along (E11), and Tie It Right (E17) are used in pack and den meetings as gathering games and other activities as needed. Become familiar with them so they can be used at a moment's notice.

Wolf and Bear activities correlate as much as possible to facilitate combining of Wolf and Bear dens.

Bear Matrix

Achievements are rotated to ensure that Cub Scouts have an opportunity to earn the Bear badge within six months. To earn the Bear the boy must complete achievements in the following categories: God (1 of 2), Country (3 of 5), Family (4 of 6), and Self (4 of 11). Additional achievements completed will be counted as electives.

Month	Achievement	Electives
January	What's Cooking (A9) Building a Model (A21)	Art (E9)
February	Take Care of Your Planet (A6) Tying It All Up (A22)	Repair (E17) Collecting Things (E22)
March	Past is Exciting and Important (A8) Information Please (A17) Jot It Down (A18)	Magic (E13)
April	Emblems of Faith (A2) Sharing Your World with Wildlife (A5) Be Ready (A11)	Space (E1) Weather (E2) Electricity (E4) Things That Go (E7)
May	What's Cooking (A9) Ride Right (A14) Games, Games, Games (A15) Building Muscles (A16)	
June	Family Fun (A10) Additional ideas are included in Summer Packets created for families. See website www.lds-Scouting.org for the packets.	Landscape (E14) Swimming (E19) Sports (E20) Maps (E23) Let's Go Camping (E25)
July	What Makes America Special? (A3) Family Outdoor Adventure (A12) Shavings and Chips (A19)	Photography (E11)
August	Sharing Your World with Wildlife (A5) Take Care of Your Plant (A6)	Weather (E2) Nature Craft (E12) Water and Conservation (E15)
September	Saving Well, Spending Well (A13) Games, Games, Games (A15) Sports, Sports, Sports (A23)	
October	Law Enforcement is a Big Job (A7) Be Ready! (A11)	
November	Ways We Worship (A1) What Makes America Special (A3)	American Indian Life (E24)
December	Tall Tales (A4) Family Fun (A10) Sawdust and Nails (A20)	Cub Scout Band (E8)

Be a Leader (A24) is best completed after the Cub Scout is a Denner and fulfills the other requirements.

Webelos

Citizen and Fitness are required activity badges for the Webelos rank. They are scheduled twice a year. Depending on the boy's birthday, the activity badge may not be covered in a den meeting but will be assigned to complete at home. Readyman and Outdoorsman are required to earn Arrow of Light but they can be earned anytime during the year. Webelos must stay on task to complete the requirements in one year. Do not expect the boys to achieve all twenty activity badges!

Month	Activity Badges	Belt Loops
January	Craftsman (Technology) Artist (Mental Skills)	Art, Hockey, Ice Skating, Marbles
February	Artist (Mental Skills) Geologist (Outdoors) Showman (Mental Skills)	Geology, Gymnastics, Music, Snow Ski and Board Sports
March	Communicator (Community)	Communicating, Computer, Disability Awareness, Video Game
April	Engineer (Technology) Scientist (Technology) Note: Complete Faith requirements for Webelos (page 50 – 51)	Astronomy, Bowling, Chess, Mathematics, Science, Table Tennis, Weather
May	**Fitness** (Physical Skills) Athlete (Physical Skills) Sportsman (Bicycling)	Baseball, Badminton, Bicycling, Fitness, Nutrition, Tennis
June	Aquanaut (Physical Skills) **Outdoorsman** (Outdoor) Traveler (Mental Skills)	Archery, BB Gun Shooting, Family Travel, Fishing, Geography, Good Manners, Map and Compass, Swimming
July	**Citizen** (Community) **Outdoorsman** (Outdoor) Family Member (Community)	Heritage, Hiking, Marbles, Photography, Wildlife Conservation
August	Naturalist (Outdoor) Forester (Outdoor)	Collecting, Golf, Horseback Riding, Wildlife Conservation
September	Sportsman (Physical Skills) Scholar (Mental Skills) **Outdoorsman** (Check progress)	Basketball, Chess, Flag Football, Kickball, Language, Mathematics, Reading and Writing, Soccer
October	**Fitness** (Physical Skills) **Readyman** (Community)	Physical Fitness, Roller Skating, Softball, Ultimate
November	**Citizen** (Community) Showman (December pack meeting)	Citizenship, Language and Culture
December	Family Member (Community) Handyman (Technology)	Heritages, Good Manners, Pet Care

To facilitate combining dens, the Webelos activities correlate as closely as possible with Bear and Wolf activities. Three activity badges including Fitness and Citizen are required for the Webelos rank. Five additional activity badges including Readyman and Outdoorsman are required for Arrow of Light. The activity badges must be from different categories. See Webelos Handbook for details.

Pack Meeting

The core values for the month are presented at pack meetings in addition to receiving awards and recognition. Boys have an opportunity to share what they have accomplished the previous month and hear what they will be working on during the coming month.

Month	Core Value	Activity
January	Positive Attitude	Ward Pinewood Derby
February	Resourcefulness	Scout Dinner
March	Compassion	Diversity Awareness / International
April	Faith	Faith in God Presentations / Missionary Speakers
May	Health and Fitness	Bike Rodeo
June	Perseverance	Rocket Launch Note: Day camp is usually during the summer months and will vary depending on the stake and council.
July	Courage	Campfire / Flag Ceremony
August	Honesty	Scout Court of Honor
September	Cooperation	Games / Annual Pack Planning Meeting
October	Responsibility	Fireman / Policeman / Be Prepared
November	Citizenship	Elected Official / Mock Election
December	Respect	Service Project / Den Skits

Parents and the entire family are encouraged to attend. Pack meetings are a family activity where children of all ages are welcome to participate.

Parents will have an opportunity to assist with the pack meetings. They can volunteer at the Annual Parent / Leader Planning meeting or at any time during the year. Each month will require additional support to facilitate an exceptional program for the Cub Scouts and their families.

LDS Guide to Scouting in the Primary

Cub Scout Annual Calendar

Date	Day	Event	Note / Holidays	Songs	Wolf	Wolf Options	Bear	Bear Options	Webelos	Belt Loops
January 2012									**Core Value --> Positive Attitude**	

Faith in God: Developing Talents (5) Make an item from wood, metal, fabric, or other material, or draw, paint, or sculpt a piece of art. Display your finished work for others to see. *** Article of Faith 9. We believe all that God has revealed, all that He does now reveal, and we believe that He will yet reveal many great and important things pertaining to the Kingdom of God.

Date	Day	Event	Note / Holidays	Songs	Wolf	Wolf Options	Bear	Bear Options	Webelos	Belt Loops
		Family	Check conflict with back-to-school dates & meetings planned in 1st & 2nd week.	The Ninth Article of Faith (128)	Cooking and Eating (A8)		What's Cooking? (A9)		Artist	
1/11/12	Wed	Den	Pinewood Derby Workshop 2: Car Weigh In	Jesus Once Was a Little Child (55)	Spare-Time Fun (E5:g)		Building a Model (A21)		Craftsman	Ice Skating Hockey
1/12/12	Thu	Pack	Pinewood Derby	If Your Happy Smiles (266) (267)	Spare-Time Fun (E5:g)		Building a Model (A21)		Craftsman	
1/25/12	Wed	Den		Teach Me To Walk in the Light (177)	Be an Artist (E12)		Art (E9)		Artist	Marbles Art
February 2012									**Core Value --> Resourcefulness**	

Faith in God: Developing Talents (3) Learn to sing, play, or lead a song from the Children's Songbook. Teach or share the song in a family home evening or at Primary. Discuss how developing talents helps prepare us for service to Heavenly Father and others. *** Article of Faith 6. We believe in the same organization that existed in the Primitive Church, namely, apostles, prophets, pastors, teachers, evangelists, and so forth.

Date	Day	Event	Note / Holidays	Songs	Wolf	Wolf Options	Bear	Bear Options	Webelos	Belt Loops
2/2/12	Thu	Combined Troop/Pack	Scout Dinner	Families Can Be Together Forever (188)	Your Flag (A2)	Display Art	What Makes America Special (A3)	Display Art	Citizen (Required for Webelos)	
2/8/12	Wed	Den		All Things Bright & Beautiful (231)	Your Living World (A7)	Start a Collection (A6)	Take Care of Your Planet (A6)	Collecting Things (E22)	Geologist	Geology
2/22/12	Wed	Den		When We Are Helping (198)	Tie It Right (E17)		Tying It All Up (A22)	Repairs (E17)	Handyman	Snow Ski & Board Gymnastics
		Family		The Sixth Article of Faith (125)	Your Living World (A7)		Take Care of Your Planet (A6)		Handyman	Music

LDS Guide to Scouting in the Primary

Cub Scout Annual Calendar

Date	Day	Event	Note / Holidays	Songs	Wolf	Wolf Options	Bear	Bear Options	Webelos	Belt Loops

March 2012 — Core Value --> Compassion

Faith in God: Serving Others (1) Read and discuss the parable of the good Samaritan (see Luke 10:30-37). Plan and complete a service project that helps a family member or neighbor. After completing the project, discuss how it helped your faith grow stronger. *** Article of Faith 3. We believe that through the Atonement of Christ, all mankind may be saved, by obedience to the laws and ordinances of the Gospel.

Date	Day	Event	Note / Holidays	Songs	Wolf	Wolf Options	Bear	Bear Options	Webelos	Belt Loops
3/1/12	Thu	Pack	Diversity Awareness and Game Night	We Are Different (263)					Communicator	Disability Awareness
3/14/12	Wed	Den		Every Star Is Different (142)	Keep Your Body Health (A3)	Making Choices (A12)	Past is Exciting and Important (A8)	Magic (E13)	Communicator	Communicating
3/28/12	Wed	Den	Check conflict with Spring breaks	I'll Walk With You (140)	Computers (E21)	Say It Right (E22)	Jot It Down (A18)		Communicator	Computers
		Family		The Third Article of Faith (123)	Keep Your Body Health (A3)		Information Please (A17)			Video Games

April 2012 — Core Value --> Faith

Faith in God: Developing Talents (4) Write a poem, story, or short play that teaches a principle of the gospel or is about Heavenly Father's creations. (Cub Scout Religious Award) *** Article of Faith 1. We believe in God, the Eternal Father, and in His Son, Jesus Christ, and in the Holy Ghost. (and) Article of Faith 8. We believe the Bible to be the word of God as far as it is translated correctly; we also believe the Book of Mormon to be the word of God.

Date	Day	Event	Note / Holidays	Songs	Wolf	Wolf Options	Bear	Bear Options	Webelos	Belt Loops
4/5/12	Thu	Pack	Speakers: Bishop & Missionaries	Faith (96)	Duty to God (A11) Faith in God		Emblems of Faith (A2)		Faith *(Requirements for Webelos)*	Table Tennis / Chess
4/11/12	Wed	Den		The World is So Lovely (233)	Know Your Home & Community (A4)	Spare Time Fun - Kites (E5)	Sharing Your World With Wildlife (A5)	Space (E1) Weather (E2)	Scientist	Science / Weather
4/25/12	Wed	Den		Choose The Right Way (160)	Be Safe at Home & on the Street (A9)	Machine Power (E8)	Be Ready (A11)	Electricity (E4)	Engineer	Mathematics / Astronomy
		Family		First Article of Faith (122) & Eighth Article of Faith (127)	Faith *(Connection)*		Be Ready (A11)	Things That Go (E7)	Faith *(Requirements for Webelos)*	

[73]

LDS Guide to Scouting in the Primary

Cub Scout Annual Calendar

May 2012

Faith in God: Learning and Living the Gospel (7) Read D&C 89. Discuss how Heavenly Father blesses us when we faithfully live the Word of Wisdom. Help plan and conduct an activity to teach the Word of Wisdom to others. *** Article of Faith 7. We believe in the gift of tongues, prophecy, revelation, visions, healing, interpretation of tongues, and so forth.

Date	Day	Event	Note / Holidays	Songs	Wolf	Wolf Options	Bear	Bear Options	Webelos	Belt Loops
							Core Value --> Health and Fitness			
5/3/12	Thu	Pack	Bike Rodeo (Ask the Boy Scout Troop to run)	Go the Second Mile (167)	Be Safe at Home & on the Street (A9)		Ride Right (A14)		Sportsman (Bicycling)	Bicycling
5/9/12	Wed	Den		The Words of Wisdom (154)	Feats of Skill (A1)		Building Muscle (A16)		Fitness *(Required for Webelos)*	Fitness / Nutrition
5/23/12	Wed	Den		Friends Are Fun (262)	Sports (E20)	Tools for Fixing and Building (A5)	Games, Games, Games (A15)		Athlete	Baseball / Soccer
		Family		The Seventh Article of Faith (126)	Cooking and Eating (A8)		What's Cooking? (A9)		Fitness *(Required for Webelos)*	School Team Sport

June 2012

Faith in God: Learning and Living the Gospel (8) Prepare a pedigree chart with your name and your parents' and grandparents' names. Prepare a family group record for your family and share a family story. Discuss how performing temple work blesses families. (Cub Scout Religious Award) *** Article of Faith 4. We believe that the first principles and ordinances of the Gospel are: first, Faith in the Lord Jesus Christ; second, Repentance; third, Baptism by immersion for the remission of sins; fourth, Laying on of hands for the gift of the Holy Ghost.

Date	Day	Event	Note / Holidays	Songs	Wolf	Wolf Options	Bear	Bear Options	Webelos	Belt Loops
							Core Value --> Perseverance			
6/7/12	Thu	Pack	Bottle Rockets / Leave No Trace	Dare To Do Right (158)	*Leave No Trace*	Grow Something (E15)	*Leave No Trace*	Landscape (E14)	Scientist	Family Travel / Good Manners
6/13/12	Wed	Den	Leave No Trace may also be covered at Day Camp	The Prophet Said to Plant a Garden (237)	Sports (E20)	Let's Go Camping (E23)	Sports (E20)	Let's Go Camping (E25)	Outdoorsman *(Required for Arrow of Light)*	Map & Compass / Geography
6/18/12 - 6/22/12	Mon - Fri	Council	Day Camp	The Fourth Article of Faith (124)	Fishing (E19)		Swimming (E19)		Aquanaut	Archery / BB Guns
		Family	Travel Packet	-	Family Fun (A10)		Family Fun (A10)	Maps (E23)	Traveler	Swimming / Fishing

LDS Guide to Scouting in the Primary

Cub Scout Annual Calendar

Date	Day	Event	Note / Holidays	Songs	Wolf	Wolf Options	Bear	Bear Options	Webelos	Belt Loops

July 2012 — Core Value --> Courage

Faith in God: Learning and Living the Gospel (5) Give an opening and a closing prayer in family home evening or at Primary. Share your feelings about how prayer protects us and helps us to stay close to Heavenly Father and the Savior. (Cub Scout Religious Award) *** Article of Faith 10. We believe in the literal gathering of Israel and in the restoration of the Ten Tribes; that Zion (the New Jerusalem) will be built upon the American continent; that Christ will reign personally upon the earth; and, that the earth will be renewed and receive its paradisiacal glory.

Date	Day	Event	Note / Holidays	Songs	Wolf	Wolf Options	Bear	Bear Options	Webelos	Belt Loops
7/5/12	Thu	Pack	Outdoor Flag Ceremony	"America"	Your Flag (A2)	Sing-Along (E11)	What Makes America Special (A3)		Citizen *(Required for Webelos)*	
7/11/12	Wed	Den		Oh, What Do You Do in the Summertime (245) *Practice*	Play a Game (E4)		Shavings and Chips (A19)		Citizen *(Required for Webelos)*	Hiking
7/25/12	Wed	Den	Go on a 3 Mile Hike	"Give" Said the Little Stream (236)	Outdoor Adventure (E18)		Photography (E11)		Outdoorsman *(Required for Arrow of Light)*	Photography
		Family			Outdoor Adventure (E18)		Family Outdoor Adventure (A12)		Family Member	Heritage

August 2012 — Core Value --> Honesty

Faith in God: Learning and Living the Gospel (6) Tell a story from the Book of Mormon that teaches about faith in Jesus Christ. Share your testimony of the Savior. (Cub Scout Religious Award) *** Article of Faith 13. We believe in being honest, true, chaste, benevolent, virtuous, and in doing good to all men; indeed, we may say that we follow the admonition of Paul—We believe all things, we hope all things, we have endured many things, and hope to be able to endure all things. If there is anything virtuous, lovely, of good report or praiseworthy, we seek after these things.

Date	Day	Event	Note / Holidays	Songs	Wolf	Wolf Options	Bear	Bear Options	Webelos	Belt Loops
8/1/12	Wed	Combined Troop/Pack	Camp in Review	Oh, What Do You Do in the Summertime (245)						Wildlife Conservation
8/8/12	Wed	Den	Leave No Trace	All Things Bright and Beautiful (231)	Start a Collection (A6)		Sharing Your World with Wildlife (A5)	Water & Soil Conservation (E15)	Naturalist	Collecting
8/22/12	Wed	Den		My Heavenly Father Loves Me (228)	Birds (E13)		Nature Craft (E12)	Weather (E2)	Forester	Golf
		Family		The Thirteenth Article of Faith (132)	Your Living World (A7)		Take Care of Your Planet (A6)			Horseback Riding

LDS Guide to Scouting in the Primary

Cub Scout Annual Calendar

September 2012

Faith in God: Developing Talents (8) List five things you can do to help around your home. Discuss the importance of obeying and honoring your parents and learning how to work. *** Article of Faith 5. We believe that a man must be called of God, by prophecy, and by the laying on of hands by those who are in authority, to preach the Gospel and administer in the ordinances thereof.

Date	Day	Event	Note / Holidays	Songs	Wolf	Wolf Options	Bear	Bear Options	Webelos	Belt Loops
									Core Value -->	Cooperation
9/6/12	Thu	Pack	Summer Time Pack Awards / Fall Kickoff	Beauty Everywhere (232)						Basketball / Chess
9/12/12	Wed	Den		A Young Man Prepared (166)	Feats of Skill (A1)	Start a Collection (A6)	Games, Games, Games (A15)		Sportsman	Flag Football / Kickball
9/26/12	Wed	Den		The Still Small Voice (106)	Sports (E20)	Foot Power (E7)	Sports, Sports, Sports (A23)		Outdoorsman *(Required for Arrow of Light)*	Soccer / Language
		Family		The Fifth Article of Faith (125)	Keep Your Body Health (A3)	Books, Books, Books (E6)	Saving Well, Spending Well (A13)		Scholar	Mathematics / Reading/Writing

October 2012

Faith in God: Learning and Living the Gospel (9) Learn to sing "Choose the Right" (Hymns, no. 239). Explain what agency is and what it means to be responsible for your choices. Discuss how making good choices has helped you develop greater faith. *** Article of Faith 2. We believe that men will be punished for their own sins, and not for Adam's transgression.

Date	Day	Event	Note / Holidays	Songs	Wolf	Wolf Options	Bear	Bear Options	Webelos	Belt Loops
									Core Value -->	Responsibility
10/4/12	Thu	Pack	Policeman or Fireman Speaker	Keep the Commandments (146)	Be Safe at Home & on the Street (A9)		Law Enforcement is a Big Job (A7)		Readyman *(Required for Arrow of Light)*	Roller Skating / Softball
10/10/12	Wed	Den	Visit Fire station or Police Station	The Second Article of Faith (122)	Be Safe at Home & on the Street (A9)	Family Alert (E16)	Be Ready! (A11)		Readyman *(Required for Arrow of Light)*	Ultimate
10/24/12	Wed	Den		Choose the Right (Hymn 239)	Know Your Home & Community (A4)	Making Choices (A12)	Law Enforcement is a Big Job (A7)		Fitness *(Required for Webelos)*	Fitness
		Family			Know Your Home & Community (A4)	Be Safe at Home & on the Street (A9)	Law Enforcement is a Big Job (A7)	Be Ready! (A11)	Fitness *(Required for Webelos)*	

LDS Guide to Scouting in the Primary

Cub Scout Annual Calendar

Date	Day	Event	Note / Holidays	Songs	Wolf	Wolf Options	Bear	Bear Options	Webelos	Belt Loops

November 2012 — Core Value --> Citizenship

Faith in God: Serving Others (8) Read the twelfth article of faith. Discuss what it means to be a good citizen and how your actions can affect others. *** Article of Faith 12. We believe in being subject to kings, presidents, rulers, and magistrates, in obeying, honoring, and sustaining the law.

Date	Day	Event	Note / Holidays	Songs	Wolf	Wolf Options	Bear	Bear Options	Webelos	Belt Loops
11/1/12	Thu	Pack	Elected Official *(if election year, hold mock election)*	My Flag, My Flag (226)	Your Flag (A2)		What Makes American Special? (A3)		Citizen *(Required for Webelos)*	Citizenship
11/14/12	Wed	Den		I'm Trying To Be Like Jesus (78)	Your Flag (A2)		What Makes American Special? (A3)		Citizen *(Required for Webelos)*	
11/28/12	Wed	Den		Book of Mormon Stories (118)	Duty to God (A11) *(Faith in God)*		Ways We Worship (A1)	Prepare for Pack Meeting - Tall Tales (A4)	Prepare for Pack meeting - Showman	Language and Culture
		Family	Thanksgiving	The Twelfth Article of Faith (131)	American Indian Lore (E11)	Your Living World (A7)	American Indian Life (E24)			

December 2012 — Core Value --> Respect

Faith in God: Serving Others (2) Write a letter to a teacher, your parents, or your grandparents telling them what you appreciate and respect about them. (Cub Scout Religious Award) *** Article of Faith 11. We claim the privilege of worshiping Almighty God according to the dictates of our own conscience, and allow all men the same privilege, let them worship how, where, or what they may.

Date	Day	Event	Note / Holidays	Songs	Wolf	Wolf Options	Bear	Bear Options	Webelos	Belt Loops
12/1/12	Sat	Ward	Primary Christmas Program	Christmas Songs	Be an Actor (E2)					Good Manners
12/6/12	Thu	Pack	The Stage is Yours!	Book of Mormon Stories (118)	Be an Actor (E2)		Tall Tales (A4)	Cub Scout Band (E8)	Showman	Heritage
12/12/12	Wed	Den	Pinewood Derby Kits Workshop 1: Car Design	Pioneer Children Were Quick to Obey (215)	Tools for Fixing and Building (A5)	Make It Yourself (E3)	Sawdust and Nails (A20)		Craftsman	Pet Care
		Family	Christmas Vacation Packet	The Eleventh Article of Faith (1+A230)	Family Fun (A10)	Pets (E14)	Family Fun (A10)		Family Member	

LDS Guide to Scouting in the Primary

January Core Value – Positive Attitude

Faith in God	**Developing Talents (5):** Make an item from wood, metal, fabric, or other material, or draw, paint, or sculpt a piece of art. Display your finished work for others to see. Art work can be displayed at the Scout banquet in February or March.	**9th Article of Faith:** We believe all that God has revealed, all that He does now reveal, and we believe that He will yet reveal many great and important things pertaining to the Kingdom of God. (Song: page 128)
Wolf	*Cooking and Eating (A8: a – e)* Spare Time Fun (E5: g – i) Be an Artist (E12: a – f)	*Cooking and Eating* is done primarily in the home. The other activities are started in den meetings and completed at home.
Bear	*What's Cooking (A9: four a – g)* Building a Model (A21: g plus 2 a – f) Art (E9: a – c)	Many of the requirements are done at home or at school. Bears will be assigned a date to bring their snack to den or pack meeting.
Webelos / Arrow of Light	Craftsman Artist	Craftsman is started in December and completed in January.
Sports / Academics	Art Belt Loop Marbles Belt Loop	Ice Skating Belt Loop Hockey Belt Loop
Pack	Ward Pinewood Derby Plan a pinewood derby clinic and race for Cub Scouts and family members who want to participate.	Provide cars for any ward members who want to participate including parents, family members, young men and young women.
Songs	Jesus Once Was a Little Child (55) Teach Me To Walk In the Light (177)	If Your Happy (266) Smiles (267)
Other Activity	Fun For The Family – Positive Attitude	Family Assignment Fun For the Family – 2I, 3M, 5C

Italics indicates a requirement that is done primarily at home.

Wolf Plan for January

Achievement 8 – Cooking and Eating a) Study the food guide (MyPlate.gov). Name some foods from each of the food groups. b) Plan meals you and your family should have for one day. List things your family should have from the food groups. c) Help fix one meal for your family. Help set the table, cook the food, and wash the dishes. d) Fix your own breakfast. Wash and put away the dishes. e) Plan, prepare, and cook an outdoor meal.	**Home Assignment:** Read pages 78 – 81. Complete requirements 8a – 8e. **Den Meeting:** Discuss 8a – Good nutrition and the food groups.
Elective 5 – Spare Time a) Make a model boat with a rubber-band propeller. b) Make or put together a model boat. c) Make or put together a model airplane. d) Make or put together a model train. e) Make a model car.	**Home Assignment:** Read pages 132 – 141. Kites (5a – 5e) can be completed when the weather is conducive to kite flying. Models including a pinewood derby car may be made in den meetings or at home.
Elective 12 – Be an Artist a) Make a freehand sketch. b) Tell a story by drawing three cartoons. c) Mix yellow and blue paints, mix yellow and red, and mix red and blue. Tell about the color. d) Help draw, paint, or color some scenery for a skit, play, or puppet show. e) Make a stencil pattern. f) Make a poster for a Cub Scout activity.	**Marbles Belt Loop** 1. Explain the rules of ringer or another marble game to your leader or adult partner. 2. Spend at least 30 minutes practicing skills to play the game of ringer or another marble game. 3. Participate in a game of marbles. Marbles is an activity to include in a game box to use when there is extra time to fill.

Pinewood Derby Clinic

During a den meeting explain rules for the pinewood derby. Show car designs and provide tips on building a car. The clinic is more important for Wolf Scouts and new Scouts who may not have attended a pinewood derby race before. Boys can build their car and even paint it during their den meetings.

Discuss having a positive attitude and good sportsmanship.

Bear Plan for January

Achievement 9 – What's Cooking? a) With an adult, bake cookies. b) With an adult, make snacks for the next den meeting. c) With an adult, prepare one part of your breakfast, one part of your lunch, and one part of your supper. d) Make a list of the 'junk foods' you eat. Discuss 'junk food' with a parent or teacher. e) Make some trail food for a hike. f) With an adult, make a dessert for your family. g) With an adult, cook something outdoors.	**Home Assignment:** Read pages 80 – 89. Do four requirements. This achievement is usually done at home. Please contact the den leader if you need assistance.
Achievement 21 – Building a Model a) Build a model from a kit. b) Build a display for one of your models. c) Pretend you are planning to change the furniture layout in one of the rooms in your home. d) Make a model of a mountain, a meadow, a canyon, or a river. e) Go and see a model of a shopping center or new building that is on display somewhere. f) Make a model of a rocket, boat, car, or plane. g) Character Connection for **Resourcefulness**.	**Home Assignment:** Read pages 156 – 161. Additional projects can be completed at home. **Den Meeting:** Complete 21g and two other requirements.
Ice Skating Belt Loop 1. Explain ways to protect yourself while ice skating and the need for proper safety equipment. 2. Spend at least 30 minutes practicing the skills of skating. 3. Go ice skating with a family member or den for at least three hours. Chart your time.	**Hockey Belt Loop** 1. Explain ways to protect yourself while skating. Demonstrate how to put on all necessary safety equipment. Explain why proper safety equipment is important. 2. Spend 30 minutes practicing the skills of hockey: skating, stick handling, passing, shooting, and checking. This may be over two different practice periods. 3. Play a game of hockey while on roller skates or hockey skates.

Webelos Plan for January

Craftsman (Technology Group)

1. Explain how to safely handle the tools that you will use for this activity badge safely.
2. With adult supervision and using hand tools, construct two different wooden objects you and your Webelos den leader agree on, such as the items listed below. Use a coping saw or jigsaw for these projects. Put them together with glue, nails, or screws. Paint or stain them.
3. Make a display stand, or box to be used to display a model or an award. Or make a frame for a photo or painting. Use suitable material.
4. Make four useful items using materials other than wood that you and your Webelos den leader agree on, such as clay, plastic, leather, metal, paper, rubber, or rope. These should be challenging items and must involve several operations.

Home Assignment:
Read pages 225 – 244.
Complete 1 through 4 for a total of three wooden projects and four items made of materials other than wood (clay, plastic, leather, metal, paper, rubber, or rope.)

Den Meeting:
Make a stand for a pinewood derby car.

Project Ideas:
Book rack, Napkin holder, Shelf, Animal cutouts, Bulletin board, Garden tool rack, Weather vane, Lid holder, Tie rack, Mailbox, Letter holder, Birdhouse, Notepad holder, Desk nameplate, Toolbox, Letter, Bill, and Pencil holder, Towel rack, Bread box, Recipe holder, Key rack, Lamp stand, Measuring cup rack, Kitchen knife rack, Measuring spoon rack, Kitchen utensil rack.

Artist (Mental Group)

1. Talk to an artist about careers in art.
2. Create a portfolio of your Artist activity badge.

Do five of the following:

3. Draw or paint an original picture out-of-doors, using the art materials you prefer.
4. List the primary and secondary colors.
5. Using a computer, make six original designs.
6. Draw a profile of a member of your family.
7. Use clay to sculpt a simple object.
8. Make a mobile, using your choice of materials.
9. Make an art construction, using your choice of materials.
10. Create a collage that expresses you.
11. While you are a Webelos, earn the Cub Scout Academics belt loop for Art.

Home Assignment:
Read pages 102 – 121.
This activity badge is done both at home and in den meetings.

Den Meeting:
Boys define projects for den meetings and share art work at the Scout dinner/pack meeting.

Art Belt Loop

1. Make a list of common materials used in art.
2. Demonstrate use of: lines, circles, dots, shapes, colors, patterns, textures, space, balance, or perspective.
3. Identify the three primary colors and the three secondary colors that can be made by mixing them. Use them to create a painting.

February Core Value – Resourcefulness

Faith in God	**Developing Talents (3):** Learn to sing, play, or lead a song from the Children's Songbook. Teach or share the song in a family home evening or at Primary. Discuss how developing talents helps prepare us for service to Heavenly Father and others.	**6th Article of Faith:** We believe in the same organization that existed in the Primitive Church, namely, apostles, prophets, pastors, teachers, evangelists, and so forth. (Song: page 125)
Wolf	*Start a Collection (A6: a – c)* *Your Living World (A7: a – f)* Tie It Right (E17: a – g)	Be an Artist started in January; art displayed in February or March. *Your Living World* is done at home.
Bear	*Take Care of Your Planet (A6: 3 a – g)* Tying It All Up (A22: 5 a – f) Repair (E17: a – e) Collecting Things (E22: a – c)	Art started in January; art work displayed in February or March. *Take Care of Your Planet* is done at home.
Webelos / Arrow of Light	Artist Geologist Showman	Art work displayed in February or March.
Sports / Academics	Geology Belt Loop Music Belt Loop	Snow Ski and Board Sports Belt Loop Gymnastics Belt Loop
Pack	Scout Dinner / Court of Honor Display art and collections / sing a song as a pack or den.	Pack participates and leads the flag ceremony.
Music	Families Can be Together Forever (188) All Things Bright and Beautiful (231) When We Are Helping (198)	Boys select a favorite song to sing at the Scout dinner.
Other Activity	Fun For The Family – Resourcefulness	Family Assignment Fun For the Family – 3A, 3F, 4O, 4P

Wolf Plan for February

Achievement 6 – Start a Collection a) Character Connection for **Positive Attitude**. b) Make a collection. Start with 10 things. Put them together in a neat way. c) Explain your collection to another person.	**Home Assignment:** Read pages 70 – 73. Start a collection (see samples on page 72). **Den Meeting:** Share collection at den and pack meeting.
Achievement 7 – Your Living World a) Character Connection for **Respect**. b) Land, air and water can get dirty. Discuss with your family ways this can happen. c) Find out how and what is recycled where you live. Find out what items you can recycle. d) Pick up litter in your neighborhood. Wear gloves to protect your hands. e) Find three stories that tell how people are protecting our world. Read and discuss. f) List three ways you can save energy; do it.	**Home Assignment:** Read pages 74 – 77. Recycle, reuse, and conserve energy at home. **Den Meeting:** Discuss recycling and how Scouts can respect the environment and commit to recycling, reusing, and conserving energy. **Den Service Project:** Pick up litter at church and school.
Elective 17 – Tie It Right a) Learn to tie an overhand knot and a square knot. b) Tie your shoelaces with a square bow knot. c) Wrap and tie a package so that it is neat and tight. d) Tie a stack of newspapers the right way. e) Tie two cords together with an overhand knot. f) Learn to tie a necktie. g) Wrap the end of a rope with tape to keep it from unwinding.	**Home Assignment:** Read pages 190 – 195. Some of the items on the list may not be as relevant as they were at one point in time. **Den Meeting:** Knots will be taught repeatedly throughout the year. Repetition is important in learning this basic Scouting skill.
Other Ideas for February include: **Music Belt Loop** 1. Explain why music is important. 2. Pick a song with two verses and learn it. 3. Listen to four different types of music.	**Snow Ski and Board Sports Belt Loop** 1. Explain planning for snow skiing or boarding. 2. Be able to explain safety and courtesy codes. 3. Go skiing or snowboarding. **Gymnastics Belt Loop** 1. Explain the six events of men's gymnastics. 2. Participate in three of the six events. 3. Explain the safety rules you should follow.

Bear Plan for February

Achievement 6 – Take Care of Your Plant a) Save 5 pounds of glass or aluminum. b) Plant a tree in your yard or community. c) Find out what happens to your trash. d) List all the ways water is used in your home. e) Discuss the kinds of energy your family uses. f) Find out about your family's use of electricity. g) Take part in a neighborhood clean-up project.	**Home Assignment:** Read pages 56 – 63. Complete three requirements.
Achievement 22 – Tying It All Up a) Whip the ends of a rope. b) Tie a square knot, bowline, sheet bend, two half hitches, and slip knot. Tell how each knot is used. c) Learn how to keep a rope from tangling. d) Coil a rope. Throw it, hitting a 2-foot square marker 20 feet away. e) Learn a magic rope trick. f) Make your own rope.	**Home Assignment:** Read pages 162 – 169. **Den and Pack Meeting:** Complete five requirements.
Elective 22 – Collecting Things Read pages 268 – 269. a) Start a stamp collection. b) Display a collection of emblems, coins, or other items to show at a pack meeting. c) Start your own library. Display art and collections at Scout dinner or at a pack meeting.	**Home Assignment:** Read pages 268 – 269. Start a new collection and determine how it will be displayed. Items need to be accurately identified and marked. **Den Meeting:** Share a new collection that you started this year.
Elective 17 – Repair a) With the help of an adult, fix an electric plug or appliance. b) Use glue or epoxy to repair something. c) Remove and clean a drain trap. d) Refinish or repaint something. e) Agree with an adult in your family on some repair job to be done and do it. (Each time you do this differently, it counts as a completed project.)	**Home Assignment:** Read pages 246 – 249. The basics are covered in the den meeting but the work is done at home. Each project is counted as an additional point towards an Arrow Point. **Den Meeting:** Basics tools and techniques are explained in the den meeting then work is done at home.

Webelos Plan for February

Showman (Mental Skill Group)
Complete six activities of your choice; these can be from any area (puppetry, music, or drama).

Puppetry Do one of these not done previously:
1. Write a puppet play about one of your Webelos activities or a subject of your choice.
2. Make a set of puppets or marionettes for the play you have written or for another play.
3. Build a simple stage for marionettes or puppets.
4. Alone or with the help of others, put on a puppet show for your den or pack.
5. Make a set of four paper bag puppets for a singing group. Sing a song with the puppets.
6. There are sock, stick, and finger puppets. There are paper bag puppets and marionettes. Explain their differences and show any puppets you have made for this badge.

Drama Do one of these not done previously:
1. Give a monologue (a talk) on a patriotic, humorous, holiday, or another subject.
2. Attend a play. Describe the story. Tell what you liked about it.
3. Read a play. Make a model stage setting for one of the acts.
4. Write, put on, and take part in a one-act play.
5. Make a list of stage directions. Explain them.
6. Describe a theater-in-the-round. What are its good and bad points?
7. Explain the difference between a grand opera and a light opera; a musical and a play.
8. Read about William Shakespeare. Draw a picture of his Globe Theater.

Music Do one of these not already done previously.
1. Play four tunes on any band or orchestra instrument. Read these from music.
2. Sing one song indoors and one song outdoors, either alone or with a group. Tell what you need to do differently when singing outdoors.
3. Make a collection of three or more records, tapes, or music CDs. Tell what you like about each.
4. Tell what folk music is. Hum, sing, or play a folk tune on a musical instrument.
5. Name three American composers. Name a famous work by each.
6. Draw a staff. Draw on it a clef, sharp, flat, natural, note, and rest. Tell what each is used for.
7. Show the difference between 2/4, 3/4, and 4/4 time by beating time or playing an instrument.
8. While you are a Webelos Scout, earn the Cub Scout Academics belt loop for Music.

Geologist (Outdoor Group)
Read pages 279 – 298.
1. Collect five geologic specimens.
2. Give examples of minerals used in products.
3. Make a scale of mineral hardness for objects found at home.
4. List some of the geologic materials used in building your home.
5. Make a drawing that shows the cause of a volcano, a geyser, or an earthquake.
6. Explain one way a mountain is formed.
7. Describe a fossil. Find two examples of fossils in your area.
8. Take a field trip to a geological site. Discuss what you learned.
9. While you are a Webelos Scout, earn the Geology belt loop

Geology Belt Loop
1. Define geology. Display collection at Scout dinner/pack meeting.
2. Collect a sample of igneous, sedimentary, and metamorphic rocks. Explain how each was formed.
3. Explain the difference between a rock and a mineral.

March Core Value – Compassion

Faith in God	**Serving Others (1):** Read and discuss the parable of the good Samaritan (see Luke 10:30–37). Plan and complete a service project that helps a family member or neighbor. After completing the project, discuss how it helped your faith grow stronger.	**3rd Article of Faith:** We believe that through the Atonement of Christ, all mankind may be saved, by obedience to the laws and ordinances of the Gospel. (Song: page 123)
Wolf	*Keep Your Body Healthy (A3: a – c)* Making Choices (A12: four g – k) Computers (E21: a – c) Say It Right (E22: a – c)	*Keeping Your Body Healthy* is done at home.
Bear	Past is Exciting and Important (A8: g, d – e) Information Please (A17: a, three b – f) Jot It Down (A18: h, plus four a – g) Magic (E13: a – d)	Having compassion for those who are different from you is important. Children learn about how to treat others when they see adults treat others with respect and compassion.
Webelos / Arrow of Light	Communicator	
Sports / Academics	Communicating Belt Loop Disability Awareness Belt Loop	Computer Belt Loop Video Game Belt Loop
Pack	Difference Awareness Trail Youth Protection	
Songs	We Are Different (263) Every Star Is Different (142) I'll Walk With You (140)	
Other Activity	Fun For The Family – Compassion	Family Assignment Fun For the Family – 1L, 2E, 4K, 5R

Wolf Plan for March

Faith in God: Learn to sing "Choose the Right" (Hymns 239). Explain what agency is and what it means to be responsible for your choices. Discuss how making good choices has helped you develop greater faith.	**Learning and Living the Gospel (9)** Sing in den meeting and discuss making choices.
Achievement 3 – Keeping Your Body Healthy a) Make a chart and keep track of your health habits for two weeks. b) Tell four ways to stop the spread of colds. c) Show what to do for a small cut on your finger.	**Home Assignment:** Read pages 36 – 59. Use a chart to track your health habits every day for two weeks. **Den Meeting:** Complete 3b and 3c; monitor chart.
Achievement 12 – Making Choices Read pages 100 – 106. a) Character Connection for **Courage**. b) Complete 12g – 12k.	**Den Meeting:** Complete 12g – 12k. Sing "Choose the Right". In October, Choices A12: b – f are covered.
Elective 21 – Computers Read pages 216 – 217. a) Visit a business where computers are used. b) Explain what a computer program does. Use a program to write a report or letter. c) Tell use of computer mouse and CD-ROM.	**Elective 22 – Say It Right** Read pages 218 – 221. a) Say "hello" in a language other than English. b) Count to ten in a language other than English. c) Tell a short story to your den. d) Tell how to get to a nearby fire station or police station from your home using directions. e) Invite a boy to join Cub Scouting.
Computer Belt Loop 1. Explain the parts of a personal computer: central processing unit (CPU), monitor, keyboard, mouse, modem, and printer. 2. Demonstrate how to start up and shut down a personal computer properly. 3. Use your computer to prepare and print a document.	**Disability Awareness Belt Loop** 1. Visit with a child or adult with special needs. Find out what this person enjoys and what this person finds difficult. 2. Attend a disabilities event and tell your leader what you thought about the experience. 3. Make a display about one or more disabilities. Share the display at a pack meeting.
Video Games Belt Loop (Completed with parents at home) 1. Explain why it is important to have a rating system for video games. Check your video games to be sure they are right for your age. 2. With an adult, create a schedule for you to do things that includes your chores, homework, and video gaming. Do your best to follow this schedule. 3. Learn to play a new video game that is approved by your parent, guardian, or teacher.	

Bear Plan for March

Achievement 8 – Past is Exciting and Important a) Visit your library or newspaper office. b) Find someone who was a Cub Scout a long time ago and talk with him. c) Add to an existing den or pack scrapbook. d) Do your genealogy and/or talk to your grandparents about when they were young. e) Find out some history about your community. f) Start your own history: keep a journal. g) Character Connection for **Respect**.	**Home Assignment:** Read pages 72 – 79. Complete 8d at home. **Den Meeting:** Complete 8g and two other requirements.
Achievement 17 – Information Please a) With an adult in your family, choose a TV show. Watch it together. b) Play a game of charades. c) Visit a newspaper office or a TV or radio station and talk to a news reporter. d) Use a computer to get information. Write a report. e) Write a letter to a company that makes something you use. f) Talk with a parent about how getting and giving facts fits into his or her job.	**Home Assignment:** Read pages 136 – 139. Complete 17a, 17d, 17e, and 17f at home. **Den Meeting:** Complete 17b and if possible 17c. Complete 17a and four other requirements.
Elective 13 – Magic a) Learn and show three magic tricks. b) With your den, put on a magic show for someone else. c) Learn and show four puzzles. d) Learn and show three rope tricks.	**Home Assignment:** Read pages 230 – 235. Practice at home. **Den Meeting:** Put on a magic show at the pack meeting.
Achievement 18 – Jot It Down a) Make a list of the things you want to do today. Check them off when you have done them. b) Write two letters to relatives or friends. c) Keep a daily record of your activities for two weeks. d) Write an invitation to someone. e) Write a thank-you note. f) Write a story about something you have done with your family. g) Write about the activities of your den. h) Character Connection for **Honesty**.	**Home Assignment:** Read pages 140 – 145. Complete 18h and four other requirements. **Den Meeting:** Complete writing project in den meeting.

Webelos Plan for March

Communicator (Community Group)

Home Assignment: **Den Meeting:** Do seven of the requirements.
Read pages 165 – 196.
1. Play the Body Language Game with your den.
2. Prepare and give a three-minute talk.
3. Invent a sign language or a picture writing language and use it to tell someone a story.
4. Identify and discuss with your den different methods of communication (at least six.)
5. Invent your own den secret code and send one of your den members a secret message.
6. With your den or your family, visit a library.
7. Visit the newsroom of a newspaper or a radio or television station.
8. Write an article about a den activity for your pack newsletter.
9. Invite a person with a visual, speaking, or hearing impairment to visit your den.
10. Invite a person who speaks another language (such as Spanish, French, Arabic, Hebrew, etc.) as well as English to visit your den.
11. Use a personal computer to write a letter to a friend or relative.
12. Search the Internet and connect to five web sites that interest you.
13. Exchange e-mail with a friend or relative.
14. Earn the Academics belt loop for Computers.
15. Earn the belt loop for Communicating.
16. Find out about jobs in communications.

Computer Belt Loop
1. Explain the parts of a personal computer: central processing unit (CPU), monitor, keyboard, mouse, modem, and printer.
2. Demonstrate how to start up and shut down a personal computer properly.
3. Use your computer to prepare and print a document.

Communicating Belt Loop
1. Tell a story or relate an incident to a group of people, such as your family, den, or members of your class.
2. Write a letter to a friend or relative.
3. Make a poster about something that interests you. Explain the poster to your den.

Volleyball Belt Loop
1. Explain the rules of volleyball to your leader or adult partner.
2. Spend at least 30 minutes practicing skills to play the sport of volleyball.
3. Participate in a volleyball game.

April Core Value – Faith

Faith in God	Developing Talents (4): Write a story, poem, or short play that teaches a principle of the gospel or is about Heavenly Father's creations. **(Cub Scout Religious Award)** Learning and Living the Gospel (2): Give a family home evening lesson on Joseph's Smith First Vision (see Joseph Smith- History 1:1-20). Discuss how Heavenly Father answers our sincere prayers. **(Cub Scout Religious Award)**	**1st Article of Faith:** We believe in God, the Eternal Father, and in His Son, Jesus Christ, and in the Holy Ghost. (Song: page 122) **8th Article of Faith:** We believe the Bible to be the word of God as far as it is translated correctly; we also believe the Book of Mormon to be the word of God. (Song: page 127)
Wolf	*Know your Home and Community (A4: a – e)* *Be Safe at Home and on the Street (A9: a – c)* Duty to God (A11: a – d)	Spare Time Fun (E5: a – f) (Kites) Machine Power (E8: a – d)
Bear	Emblems of Faith (A2) *Sharing Your World w/ Wildlife (A5: a – e)* *Be Ready! (A11: a – g)*	Space (E1: a – f) Weather (E2: a – f) Electricity (E4: a – c) Things That Go (E7: a – d)
Webelos / Arrow of Light	Engineer Scientist	Faith Requirements for Webelos Rank
Sports / Academics	Astronomy Belt Loop Science Belt Loop Mathematics Belt Loop Weather Belt Loop	Bowling Belt Loop Table Tennis Belt Loop Chess Belt Loop
Pack	Special speaker (missionaries, bishop, etc.) How Faith in God inspires them in their everyday life. Prepare a skit, story, or poem that teaches a principle of the gospel.	Faith in God presentations (Youth) and On My Honor (Adults)
Songs	Faith (96) The World is So Lovely (233)	Choose The Right Way (160)
Other Activity	Fun For The Family – Faith	Family Assignment Fun For the Family – 1D, 3B, 4D

Wolf Plan for April

Achievement 4 – Know Your Home and Community a) Make a list of phone numbers you need in case of an emergency. Put a copy of this list by each phone or in a central place in your home. b) Tell what to do if someone comes to the door and wants to come in. c) Tell what to do if someone calls on the phone. d) When you and your family leave home, remember to. e) Talk with your family members. Make and use job chart for one month. f) Visit an important place in your community, such as a historic or government location.	**Home Assignment:** Read pages 60 – 63. Complete 4a – 4e; discuss in a den meeting then completed at home. Phone lists and checklist are in Wolf Handbook. If completed previously, verify that the information is still correct. **Den Meeting:** Walk through downtown and take pictures of Police Station, Fire Station, and Post Office.
Achievement 9 – Be Safe at Home and On the Street a) Character Connection for **Responsibility.** b) With an adult check, your home for hazards and know how to make your home safe. c) Check your home for danger from fire. d) Practice good rules of street and road safety. e) Know the rules of bike safety.	**Home Assignment:** Read pages 82 – 87. Complete 9a –9c. **Den Meeting:** Discuss or review 9a – 9c. Bike safety is covered at bike rodeo which is held in the spring.
Achievement 11 – Duty to God a) Character Connection for **Faith.** b) Talk with your family about what they believe. c) Give two ideas on how you can practice or demonstrate your religious beliefs. d) Find out how you can help your church.	**Home Assignment:** Read pages 94 – 99. Complete 11b and 11c. **Den Meeting:** Complete 11a – Discuss Joseph Smith and early Mormon pioneers.
Elective 5 – Spare Time Fun (Kites) Read pages 132 – 138. a) Explain safety rules for kite flying. b) Make and fly a paper bag kite. c) Make and fly a two-stick kite. d) Make and fly a three-stick kite. e) Make and use a reel for kite string.	**Elective 8 – Machine Power** Read pages 148 – 151. a) Name 10 kinds of trucks, construction machinery, or farm machinery and tell what each is used for. b) Help an adult do a job using a wheel and axle. c) Show how to use a pulley. d) Make and use a windlass.

Bear Plan for April

Achievement 2 – Emblems of Faith Complete the requirement for **Faith in God**.	**Home Assignment:** Read pages 30 – 33.
Achievement 5 – Sharing Your World with Wildlife a) Choose a bird or animal that you like and find out how it lives. Make a poster. b) Build or make a bird feeder or birdhouse. c) Explain a wildlife conservation officer. d) Visit one of the following: Zoo, Nature center, Aviary, Wildlife refuge, Game preserve. e) Name one animal that has become extinct in the last 100 years.	**Home Assignment:** Read pages 50 – 55. **Den Meeting:** Complete four requirements.
Achievement 11 – Be Ready! a) Tell what to do in case of an accident in the home when a family member needs help. b) Tell what to do in case of a water accident. c) Tell what to do in case of a school bus accident. d) Tell what to do in case of a car accident. e) With your family, plan escape routes from your home and have a practice drill. f) Have a health checkup by a physician. g) Character Connection for **Courage**.	**Home Assignment:** Read pages 96 – 105. After den meeting, share what your Scout has learned with the entire family. Complete 11e practice an escape route. **Den Meeting:** Discuss and reenact accidents using right and wrong ways to react in each situation. Complete 11a, 11b, 11c, 11d, and 11g.
Elective 1 – Space a. Identify two constellations and the North Star. b. Make pinhole planetarium, show constellations. c. Visit a planetarium. d. Build a model of a rocket or space satellite. e. Read and talk about at least one man-made satellite and one natural one. f. Find a picture of another planet in our solar system. Explain how it is different from Earth.	**Elective 2 – Weather** 1. Learn how to read an outdoor thermometer. 2. Build a weather vane. 3. Make a rain gauge. 4. Find out what a barometer is; how it works. 5. Learn to identify three different kinds of clouds. Estimate their heights. 6. Watch the weather forecast on TV every day for two weeks.
Elective 4 – Electricity a. Wire a buzzer or doorbell. b. Make an electric buzzer game. c. Make a simple bar or horseshoe electromagnet. d. Use a simple electric motor. e. Make a crane with an electromagnetic lift.	**Elective 7 – Things That Go** a. With an adult's help, make a scooter or a Cubmobile. Know the safety rules. b. With an adult's help, make a windmill. c. With an adult's help, make a waterwheel. d. Make an invention of your own design that goes.

Webelos Plan for April

Faith Requirements for Webelos Rank
a. Know: Tell what you have learned about faith.
b. Commit: Tell how these faith experiences help you live your duty to God. Name one faith practice that you will continue to do in the future.
c. Practice: After doing these requirements, tell what you have learned about your beliefs.

Do two of the following:
- Attend the mosque, church, synagogue, temple, or other religious organization of your choice, talk with your religious leader about your beliefs. Tell your family and your Webelos den leader what you learned.
- Discuss with your family and Webelos den leader how your religious beliefs fit in with the Scout Oath and Scout Law, and what character-building traits your religious beliefs have in common with the Scout Oath and Scout Law.
- With your religious leader, discuss and make a plan to do two things you think will help you draw nearer to God. Do these things for a month.
- For at least a month, pray or meditate reverently each day as taught by your family, and by your church, temple, mosque, synagogue, or religious group.
- Under the direction of your religious leader, do an act of service for someone else. Talk about your service with your family and Webelos den leader. Tell them how it made you feel.
- List at least two ways you believe you have lived according to your religious beliefs.

Engineer (Technology Group)
Read p. 211 – 226.
1. Talk to an engineer, surveyor, or architect in your area about the jobs in engineering.
2. Draw a floor plan of your house. Include doors, windows, and stairways.

Do four of the following:
3. Visit a construction job. Look at a set of plans used to build the facility.
4. Visit a civil engineer or surveyor to learn how to measure the length of a property line.
5. Tell about how electricity is generated and then gets to your home.
6. Construct a simple working electrical circuit using a flashlight battery, a switch, and light.
7. Make drawings of three kinds of bridges and explain their differences.
8. Make a simple crane using a block and tackle.
9. Build a catapult and show how it works.
10. Earn the belt loop for Mathematics.

Scientist (Technology Group)
Read p. 401 – 428.
1. Read Bernoulli's Principle. Show how it works.
2. Read Pascal's Law. Tell about some inventions that use Pascal's law.
3. Read Newton's first law of motion. Show in three different ways how inertia works.
4. Earn the Science belt loop.

Do six of the following:
5. Show the effects of atmospheric pressure.
6. Show the effects of air pressure.
7. Show the effects of water pressure.
8. Build and launch a model rocket.
9. Explain fog. Show how it works.
10. Explain how crystals are formed. Make some.
11. Explain center of gravity to keep your balance.
12. Show in three ways your eyes work together.
13. Earn the Weather belt loop.
14. Earn the Astronomy belt loop.

Belt Loop Options for April

Astronomy Belt Loop 1. Set up and demonstrate how to focus a simple telescope or binoculars. 2. Draw a diagram of our solar system--identify the planets and other objects. 3. Explain the following terms: planet, star, solar system, galaxy, the Milky Way, black hole, red giant, white dwarf, comet, meteor, moon, asteroid, and universe.	**Science Belt Loop** 1. Explain the scientific method to your adult partner. 2. Use the scientific method in a simple science project. Explain the results to an adult. 3. Visit a museum, a laboratory, an observatory, a zoo, an aquarium, or other facility that employs scientists. Talk to a scientist about his or her work.
Mathematics Belt Loop 1. Do five activities within your home or school that require the use of mathematics. Explain to your den how you used everyday math. 2. Keep track of the money you earn and spend for three weeks. 3. Measure five items using both metric and non metric measures. Find out about the history of the metric system of measurement.	**Weather Belt Loop** 1. Make a poster that shows and explains the water cycle. 2. Set up a simple weather station to record rainfall, temperature, air pressure, or evaporation for one week. 3. Watch the weather forecast on a local television station.
Bowling Belt Loop 1. Explain to your leader or adult partner the rules of courtesy and safety for bowling. 2. Show how to pick out a ball of proper weight and with finger holes that fit your hand. 3. Play a complete game with your family or den.	**Table Tennis Belt Loop** 1. Explain the rules of table tennis to your leader or adult partner. 2. Spend at least 30 minutes practicing table tennis skills. 3. Participate in a table tennis game.
Chess Belt Loop 1. Identify the chess pieces and set up a chess board for play. 2. Demonstrate the moves of each chess piece to your den leader or adult partner. 3. Play a game of chess. (For a rainy April)	

May Core Value – Health and Fitness

Faith in God	**Learning and Living the Gospel (7):** Read D&C 89. Discuss how Heavenly Father blesses us when we faithfully live the Word of Wisdom. Help plan and conduct an activity to teach the Word of Wisdom to others.	**7th Article of Faith:** We believe in the gift of tongues, prophecy, revelation, visions, healing, interpretation of tongues, and so forth. (Song: page 126)
Wolf	Feats of Skill (A1: a – e plus one f – l) Tools for Fixing and Building (A5: a – e) *Be Safe at Home and on Streets (A9: d – e)* Bike safety is part of the pack meeting bike rodeo. (May is National Bike Safety Month.)	*Cooking and Eating (A8: a – e)* Sports (E20: h – m; o)
Bear	Ride Right (A14: a plus three b – g) Games, Games, Games (A15: a – c) Building Muscles (A16: a – b)	*What's Cooking (A9: four a – g) Cub Scouts do this achievement at home. If parents need assistance, please contact the den leader.*
Webelos / Arrow of Light	**Fitness** Athlete Sportsman (Bicycling)	
Sports / Academics	Nutrition Belt Loop Fitness Belt Loop Bicycling Belt Loop	Baseball Belt Loop Badminton Belt Loop Tennis Belt Loop
Pack	Bike Rodeo	Request assistance from the Boy Scouts in the troop or team.
Songs	Go the Second Mile (167) The Words of Wisdom (154) Friends Are Fun (262)	
Other Activity	Memorial Day Parade Fun For The Family – Health and Fitness	Family Assignment Fun For the Family – 1H, 2C, 4A

Wolf Plan for May

Achievement 1 – Feats of Skill Read pages 38 – 45. a) Play catch with someone 10 steps away. b) Walk a line back and forth. c) Do a front roll. d) Do a back roll. e) Do a falling forward roll. Do one of the following: f) See how high you can jump. g) Do the elephant walk, frog leap, and crab walk. h) Using a basic swim stroke, swim 25 feet. i) Tread water for 15 seconds. j) Using a basketball or playground ball, do a Chest pass, Bounce pass, Overhand Pass k) Do a frog stand. l) Run or jog in place for 5 minutes.	**Achievement 8 – Cooking and Eating** Read pages 78 – 81. a) Study the food guideline at MyPlate.gov. Name foods from each food groups. b) Plan meals you and your family should have for one day. List things your family should have from the food groups. c) Help fix one meal for your family. Set the table, cook the food, and wash the dishes. d) Fix your own breakfast. Wash and put away the dishes. e) Plan, prepare, and cook an outdoor meal.
Achievement 5 – Tools for Fixing and Building Read pages 64 – 69. a) Point out and name seven tools. Do this at home, or go to a hardware store with an adult. Tell what each tool does. b) Show how to use pliers. c) Identify a Philips head and a standard screw. Then use the right tool to drive and then remove one from a board. d) Show how to use a hammer. e) Make something else useful. (Idea: Make a present for Father's Day)	**Elective 20 – Sports** Read pages 196 – 197. h) Show how to make a sprint start in track. See how far you can run in 10 seconds. i) Do a standing long jump. j) Play a game of flag football. k) Show how to dribble and kick a soccer ball. l) Play a game of baseball or softball. m) Show how to shoot, pass, and dribble a basketball. Take part in a game.
Achievement 9 – Be Safe at Home and On the Street Read pages 82 – 87. Complete requirements 9a – 9e. a) Character Connection for **Responsibility.** b) Check your home for hazards and know how to make your home safe. c) Check your home for danger from fire. d) Practice good rules of street and road safety. e) Know the rules of bike safety.	**Nutrition Belt Loop** 1. Make a poster of foods that are good for you. Share the poster with your den. 2. Explain the difference between a fruit and a vegetable. Eat one of each. 3. Help prepare and eat a healthy meal of foods that are included on My Plate. With your parent's or adult partner's permission, see www.myplate.gov

Bear Plan for May

Achievement 9 – What's Cooking? Read pages 80 – 89. Do four requirements: a) With an adult, bake cookies. b) With an adult, make snacks for the next den meeting. c) With an adult, prepare one part of your breakfast, one part of your lunch, and one part of your supper. d) Make a list of the 'junk foods' you eat. Discuss 'junk food' with a parent or teacher. e) Make some trail food for a hike. f) With an adult, make a dessert for your family. g) With an adult, cook something outdoors.	**Bicycling Belt Loop** 1. Explain the rules of safe bicycling to your den leader or adult partner. 2. Demonstrate how to wear the proper safety equipment for bicycling. 3. Show how to ride a bike safely. Ride for at least half an hour with an adult partner, family, or den.
Achievement 14 – Ride Right Read pages 118 – 125. a) Know the rules for bike safety. b) Learn to ride a bike, if you have not by now. c) Keep your bike in good shape. Identify the parts of a bike that should be checked often. d) Change a tire on a bicycle. e) Protect your bike from theft. Use a lock. f) Ride a bike for 1 mile without rest. g) Plan and take a family bike hike.	**Fitness Belt Loop** 1. Give a short report to your den or family on the dangers of drugs and alcohol. 2. Practice finding your pulse and counting your heart beats per minute. Determine your target heart rate. 3. Practice five physical fitness skills regularly. Improve performance in each skill over a month. Skills could include pull-ups, curl-ups, the standing long jump, the 50-yard dash, and the softball throw.
Achievement 15 – Games, Games, Games Read pages 126 – 129. Do two requirements: a) Set up the equipment and play any two of these outdoor games with your family or friends: Backyard golf, Badminton, Croquet, Sidewalk shuffleboard, Kickball, Softball, Tetherball, Horseshoes, and Volleyball. b) Play two organized games with your den. c) Select a game that your den has never played. Explain the rules. Tell them how to play it, and then play it with them.	**Achievement 16 – Building Muscles** Read pages 130 – 135. Do all three requirements: a) Do physical fitness stretching exercises. Then do curl-ups, push-ups, the standing long jump, and the softball throw. b) With a friend about your size, compete in at least six different two-person contests. (See examples in the Bear Handbook.) c) Compete with your den or pack in the crab relay, gorilla relay, 30-yard dash, and kangaroo relay.

Webelos Plan for May

Fitness (Physical Group) Required for Webelos 1. Character Connection for **Health and Fitness**. Explain good sportsmanship. 2. With your parents, complete a safety notebook; describe "How to Protect Your Child from Child Abuse." 3. With parents plan a week of meals. 4. Track meals and snacks for one week. 5. Discuss harmful effects of tobacco with family. 6. Discuss the effects of alcohol with your family. 7. Discuss harmful effects of drugs with family. 8. Read BSA booklet "Choose to Refuse" and discuss with an adult.	**Home Assignment:** Read pages 245 – 258. Complete 1 and six of the remaining seven requirements. Note: The *Fitness* and *Citizen* activity badges are covered twice each year to ensure all boys have the opportunity to reach Webelos within their first six months. **Baseball Belt Loop** 1. Explain the rules of baseball to your leader or adult partner. 2. Spend at least 30 minutes practicing baseball skills. 3. Participate in a baseball game.
Athlete (Physical Group) 1. Character Connection for **Perseverance**. Do all of the following: 2. Explain physically and mentally health. 3. Explain what you do to stay healthy. 4. Every time you exercise, start with at least 5 minutes of stretching warm-up activities. 5. Do as many as you can: curl-ups, pull-ups, push-ups, long jump, and ½ mile run. Show improvement in 30 days. Do two of these (show improvement in 30 days): 6. Do a vertical jump. 7. Do a 50 yard dash. 8. Ride a bike 1 mile. 9. Swim a quarter mile in a pool or lake.	**Sportsman – Bicycling (Physical Group)** Read pages 456 – 460. 1. Show the signals used by officials in one of these sports: football, basketball, baseball, soccer, or hockey. 2. Explain what good sportsmanship means. 3. Earn Cub Scout Sports belt loop for two individual sports. 4. Earn Cub Scout Sports belt loop for two team sports. Individual sports include: Badminton, Bicycling, Bowling, Fishing, Golf, Gymnastics, Ice Skating, Marbles, Physical Fitness, Roller Skating, Snow Ski and Board Sports, Swimming, Table Tennis, or Tennis. Team sports include Baseball, Basketball, Soccer, Softball, Volleyball, Flag Football, and Ultimate.
Badminton Belt Loop 1. Explain the rules of badminton to your leader or adult partner. 2. Spend at least 30 minutes practicing badminton skills. 3. Participate in a badminton game.	**Tennis Belt Loop** 1. Explain the rules of tennis to your leader or adult partner. 2. Spend at least 30 minutes practicing tennis skills. 3. Participate in a tennis game.

June Core Value – Perseverance

Faith in God	**Learning and Living the Gospel (8):** Prepare a pedigree chart with your name and your parents' and grandparents' names. Prepare a family group record for your family and share a family story. Discuss how performing temple work blesses families. **(Cub Scout Religious Award)**	4th Article of Faith: We believe that the first principles and ordinances of the Gospel are: first, Faith in the Lord Jesus Christ; second, Repentance; third, Baptism by immersion for the remission of sins; fourth, Laying on of hands for the gift of the Holy Ghost. (Song: page 124)
Wolf	Day Camp Swimming (A1: h – i) Fishing (E19: a – f) Sports (E20: c, n) Let's Go Camping (E23: e)	*Family Fun (A10: a plus two b – g)* Grow Something (E15: a – e)
Bear	Day Camp Swimming (E19: a – e) Sports (E20: a) Let's Go Camping (E25: a – b, f)	*Family Fun (A10: a – b)* Landscape (E14: a – d) Maps (E23: a – e)
Webelos / Arrow of Light	Day Camp **Outdoorsman** (Required for Arrow of Light) Aquanaut	*Traveler*
Sports / Academics	Archery Belt Loop BB Guns Belt Loop Fishing Belt Loop Swimming Belt Loop	Family Travel Belt Loop Geography Belt Loop Good Manners Belt Loop Map and Compass Belt Loop
Pack	Bottle Rockets	See special packet on Making a Bottle Rocket; requires a bottle rocket launcher which can be made at home.
Songs	Dare To Do Right (158) The Prophet Said to Plant a Garden (237)	
Other Activity	Fun For The Family – Perseverance	Family Assignment Fun For the Family – 2M, 3P, 5L

If is recommended that **Leave No Trace** be reviewed prior to attending day camp. Supplement information in summertime packets (Traveler, Outdoor Scouting, Nature, and Conservation) is available to assist in completing achievements and elective requirements over the summer.

Wolf Plan for June

Achievement 10 – Family Fun a) Character Connection for **Cooperation**. b) Make a game and play it with your family. c) Plan a walk. Go to a park or a wooded area, or visit a zoo or museum with your family. d) Read a book or Boys' Life magazine with your family. Take turns reading aloud. e) Decide with Akela, what you will watch on television or listen to on the radio. f) Attend a concert, a play, or other live program with your family. g) Have a family board game night at home with members of your family.	**Home Assignment:** Read pages 88 – 93. Complete requirements 10a plus two requirements 10b through 10g.
Achievement 1 – Feats of Skill (Swimming) h) Using a basic swim stroke, swim 25 feet. i) Tread water for 15 seconds.	**Home Assignment:** Read pages 38 – 45.
Day camp offers a variety of achievements, electives, and belt loops. The requirements offered may be different each year. The timing of day camp may also vary depending on the stake, district, or council. Summer is an ideal time for boys to pass off a variety of fun activities with their families.	
Elective 19 – Fishing (Day Camp) Read pages 200 – 203. a) Identify five different kinds of fish. b) Rig a pole with the right kind of line and hook. Attach a bobber and sinker. Go fishing. c) Bait your hook and try to catch a fish. d) Know the rules of safe fishing. e) Tell about some of the fishing laws. f) Show how to use a rod and reel.	**Elective 20 – Sports** Read pages 204 – 215. e) Earn Archery belt loop. n) Earn BB-gun Shooting belt loop. o) Participate in four outdoor physical fitness-related activities. Note: Sport activities offered at day camp may vary each year.
Elective 23 – Let's Go Camping Read pages 222 – 225. a) Explain the basics of how to take care of yourself in the outdoors. b) Tell what to do if you get lost. c) Explain the buddy system. d) Attend day camp in your area. g) Participate with your den at a campfire in front of your pack.	**Elective 15 – Grow Something** Read pages 184 – 187. a) Plant and raise a box garden. b) Plant and raise a flower bed. c) Grow a plant indoors. d) Plant and raise vegetables. e) Visit a botanical garden or other agricultural exhibition in your area.

LDS Guide to Scouting in the Primary

Bear Plan for June

Elective 20 – Sports (Day Camp) Read pages 260 – 261. a) In archery, know the safety rules and how to shoot correctly. Put six arrows into a 4-foot target at a distance of 15 feet. Other sports including Outdoor Skating (pages 263 – 264) and Track and Field events (pages 264 – 265) may be completed by the Scout but are not usually an activity at day camp.	**Elective 25 – Let's Go Camping (Day Camp)** Read pages 276 – 278. a) Learn about the ten essential items you need for a hike or campout. b) Go on a short hike with your den, following the buddy system. c) Participate with your den in front of the pack at a campfire. f) Attend day camp in your area. h) Earn the Cub Scout Leave No Trace award.

Elective 19 – Swimming (Day Camp)
Read pages 254 – 259.
a) Jump feet first into water over your head, swim 25 feet on the surface, stop, turn sharply, and swim back.
b) Swim on your back, the elementary backstroke, for 30 feet.
c) Rest by floating on your back, using as little motion as possible for at least one minute.
d) Tell what is meant by the buddy system. Know the basic rules of safe swimming.
e) Do a racing dive from edge of pool and swim 60 feet, using a racing stroke. (You might need to make a turn.)

Achievement 10 – Family Fun a) Go on a day trip or evening out with members of your family. b) Have a family fun night at home.	**Home Assignment:** Read pages 90 – 95. Complete both requirements.

Elective 14 – Landscape
Read pages 236 – 237.
a) Take care of your lawn or flower beds. Get rid of weeds. Pick up litter.
b) Make a sketch of a landscape plan for the area right around your home.
c) Take part in a project with your family or pack to make your neighborhood or community beautiful.
d) Build a greenhouse and grow twenty plants from seed.

Elective 23 – Maps
Read pages 270 – 271.
a) Look up your state on a U.S. map. What other states touch its borders?
b) Find your city or town on a map of your state. How far do you live from the state capital?
c) In which time zone do you live? How many time zones are there in the U.S.?
d) Make a map showing the route from your home to your school or den meeting place.
e) Mark a map showing the way to a place you would like to visit that is at least 50 miles from your home.

Webelos Plan for June

Traveler (Mental Group)
1. On a map or timetable from a railroad, bus line, airline, subway, or light rail, look up places to go.
2. Use a timetable to plan a trip from your home to a city in another state by railroad, bus, airline, ferry.
3. Use a map site on the Internet to plan a trip from your home to a nearby place of interest.
4. Take a trip to a place that interests you. Go by car, bus, boat, train, or plane.
5. Figure the costs per mile for the trip you took or planned to fulfill requirement 2, 4, 6, or 7.
6. Decide on four nearby trips you would like to take. Draw the route of each trip on a highway map. Using the map, act as navigator on one of these trips.
7. Decide on a trip you would like to take that lasts at least two days. Pack everything you would need for that trip.
8. Check the first aid kit in the family car.
9. Look at a map legend on a road map.
10. On a road map of your area, find a place of interest, and draw two different routes between it and your home.
11. Make a list of safety precautions you, as a traveler, should take for travel.
12. Earn the Geography belt loop.
13. Earn the Map and Compass belt loop.

Home Assignment:
Read pages 225 – 244.
Complete 1 through 6 and two of the remaining seven requirements.

Den Meeting:
Review what was learned as a family member.

Map and Compass Belt Loop
1. Show how to orient a map. Find three landmarks on the map.
2. Explain how a compass works.
3. Draw a map of your neighborhood. Label the streets; plot a route you take to get to a place that you visit often.

Family Travel Belt Loop
1. Make a list of things you would take on a three-day trip with your family then pack these items in a bag or suitcase.
2. With an adult's help, figure out the cost and miles to complete a trip to a place of interest using the family car or public transportation.
3. Research five places to visit during a trip to a place of interest. Explain to your family what you learned.

Geography Belt Loop
1. Draw a map of your neighborhood. Show natural and manmade features. Include a key or legend of map symbols.
2. Learn about the physical geography of your community. Identify the major landforms within 100 miles. Discuss with an adult what you learned.
3. Use a world globe or map to locate the continents, the oceans, the equator, and the northern and southern hemispheres. Learn how longitude and latitude lines are used to locate a site.

Good Manners Belt Loop
1. Make a poster that lists five good manners that you want to practice. Share your poster with your den or family.
2. Introduce two people correctly and politely. Be sure that one of them is an adult.
3. Write a thank-you note to someone who has given you something or done something nice for you.

Webelos Plan for June (Continued)

Outdoorsman (Outdoor Group)	Aquanaut (Physical Group)
Required for Arrow of Light, Read pages 343 – 364. Do two of these: 1. Present yourself to your Webelos den leader, properly dressed, as you would be for an overnight campout. 2. Help plan and take part in an evening outdoor activity that includes a campfire. 3. Sleep in a tent that you have helped pitch. Do five of the following: 5. Discuss Leave No Trace Frontcountry. 6. Participate in an outdoor conservation project. 7. Discuss the rules of outdoor fire safety. Using these rules, show how to build a safe fire and put it out. 8. On an outdoor activity, assist in preparing, cooking, and cleanup for one meal. *Note: Scouts are not required to go camping to achieve the Arrow of Light rank. Boys may camp with their parents or go on a day hike.* 9. Go on one 3-mile hike. 10. Whip and fuse the ends of a rope. 11. Demonstrate setting up a tent or dining fly using two half hitches and a taut-line hitch. Show how to tie a square knot and explain how it is used. 12. Visit a nearby Boy Scout camp.	Read pages 83 – 100. 1. Jump into water over your head. Come to the surface and swim 100 feet, at least half of this using a backstroke. 2. Float on your back and your front. 3. Wearing the PFD, jump into water over your head. Show how the PFD keeps your head up. Do three of these: 4. Do a front surface dive and swim under water. 5. Explain the four basic water rescue methods. 6. Show that you know how to handle a rowboat. 7. Pass the BSA "Swimmer" test. 8. Earn the Swimming belt loop. **Swimming Belt Loop** 1. Explain the rules of Safe Swim Defense. Emphasize the buddy system. 2. Play a recreational game in the water with your den, pack, or family. 3. While holding a kick board, propel yourself 25 feet using a flutter kick across the shallow end of the swimming area. **Fishing Belt Loop** 1. Review your local fishing regulations with your leader or adult partner. Explain why they are important, and commit to following them. 2. Demonstrate how to properly bait a hook. 3. Try to catch a fish.
Archery Belt Loop (Day Camp) 1. Explain the rules for safe archery that you have learned in the district/council camp or activity you are attending. 2. Demonstrate to your leader or adult partner good archery shooting techniques, including the stance and how to nock the arrow, establish the bow, draw, aim, release, follow through and retrieve arrows. 3. Practice shooting at your district or council camp for the time allowed.	**BB Gun Shooting Belt Loop (Day Camp)** 1. Explain the rules of safe BB gun shooting you have learned to your leader or adult partner. 2. Demonstrate to your leader or adult partner good BB gun shooting techniques, including eye dominance, shooting shoulder, breathing, sight alignment, trigger squeeze, follow through. 3. Practice shooting at your district or your council camp in the time allowed.

Leave No Trace

Leave No Trace is a plan that helps people to be more concerned about their environment and to help them protect it for future generations. Leave No Trace applies in a backyard or local park (frontcountry) as much as it does in the wilderness (backcountry). We should practice Leave No Trace in our attitude and actions-- wherever we go. Understanding nature strengthens our respect toward the environment. One person with thoughtless behavior or one shortcut on a trail can spoil the outdoor experience for others. Help protect the environment by remembering that while you are there, you are a visitor. When you visit the outdoors, take special care of the area. Leave everything just as you find it. Hiking and camping without a trace are signs of a considerate outdoorsman who cares for the environment. Travel lightly on the land.

Cub Scouting's Leave No Trace Awareness Award

	Cub Scout and Webelos		Cub Scout Leader
1	Discuss with your leader or parent the importance of the Leave No Trace frontcountry guidelines.	1	Discuss with your den's Cub Scouts or your pack's leaders the importance of the Leave No Trace frontcountry guidelines.
2	On three separate outings, practice the frontcountry guidelines of Leave No Trace.	2	On three separate outings demonstrate and practice the frontcountry guidelines of Leave No Trace.
3	✓Wolf Cub Scouts complete Your Living World Requirement 7. ✓Bear Cub Scouts complete, Family Outdoor Adventures Requirement 12. ✓Webelos Scouts earn the Outdoorsman activity badge.	3	Participate in presenting a den, pack, district, or council awareness session on Leave No Trace frontcountry guidelines.
4	Participate in a Leave No Trace-related service project.	4	Participate in a Leave No Trace-related service project.
5	Promise to practice the Leave No Trace frontcountry guidelines by signing the Cub Scout Leave No Trace Pledge.	5	Commit yourself to the Leave No Trace frontcountry guidelines by signing the Cub Scout Leave No Trace Pledge.
6	Draw a poster to illustrate the Leave No Trace frontcountry guidelines and display it at a pack meeting.	6	Assist at least three boys in earning Cub Scouting's Leave No Trace Awareness Award.

LDS Guide to Scouting in the Primary

Leave No Trace Guidelines for Cub Scouts

PLAN AHEAD

Watch for hazards and follow all the rules of the park or outdoor facility. Remember proper clothing, sunscreen, hats, first aid kits, and plenty of drinking water. Use the buddy system. Make sure you carry your family's name, phone number, and address.

STICK TO TRAILS

Stay on marked trails whenever possible. Short-cutting trails causes the soil to wear away or to be packed, which eventually kills trees and other vegetation. Trampled wildflowers and vegetation take years to recover. Stick to trails!

MANAGE YOUR PET

Managing your pet will keep people, dogs, livestock, and wildlife from feeling threatened. Make sure your pet is on a leash or controlled at all times. Do not let your pet approach or chase wildlife. When animals are chased or disturbed, they change eating patterns and use more energy that may result in poor health or death. Take care of your pet's waste. Take a small shovel or scoop and a pick-up bag to pick up your pet's waste— wherever it's left. Place the waste bags in a trash can for disposal.

LEAVE WHAT YOU FIND

When visiting any outdoor area, try to leave it the same as you find it. The less impact we each make, the longer we will enjoy what we have. Even picking flowers denies others the opportunity to see them and reduces seeds, which means fewer plants next year. Use established restrooms. Graffiti and vandalism have no place anywhere, and they spoil the experience for others. Leave your mark by doing an approved conservation project.

RESPECT OTHER VISITORS

Expect to meet other visitors. Be courteous and make room for others. Control your speed when biking or running. Pass with care and let others know before you pass. Avoid disturbing others by making noise or playing loud music. Respect "No Trespassing" signs. If property boundaries are unclear, do not enter the area.

TRASH YOUR TRASH

Make sure all trash is put in a bag or trash receptacle. Trash is unsightly and ruins everyone's outdoor experience. Your trash can kill wildlife. Even materials, such as orange peels, apple cores and food scraps, take years to break down and may attract unwanted pests that could become a problem.

Cub Scout Leave No Trace Pledge

I promise to practice the Leave No Trace
Frontcountry guidelines wherever I go:

1. Plan ahead
2. Stick to trails
3. Manage my pet
4. Leave what I find
5. Respect other visitors
6. Trash my trash

July Core Value – Courage

Faith in God	**Learning and Living the Gospel (5):** Give an opening and a closing prayer in family home evening or at Primary. Share your feelings about how prayer protects us and helps us to stay close to Heavenly Father and the Savior. **(Cub Scout Religious Award)**	**10th Article of Faith**: We believe in the literal gathering of Israel and in the restoration of the Ten Tribes; that Zion (the New Jerusalem) will be built upon the American continent; that Christ will reign personally upon the earth; and, that the earth will be renewed and receive its paradisiacal glory. (Song: page 128)
Wolf	Your Flag (A2: a – g) *Outdoor Adventure (E18: a – h)*	Play a Game (E4: a – f)) Sing-Along (E11: a – f)
Bear	What Makes America Special? (A3: h, i) *Family Outdoor Adventure (A12: a – e)* Shavings and Chips (A19: a – c)	Photography (E11: a – d)
Webelos / Arrow of Light	**Citizen** (Required for Webelos) **Outdoorsman** (Required for Arrow of Light) *Family Member*	Webelos can continue to work on Outdoorsman, Naturalist, and Forester which are often started at day camp.
Sports / Academics	Photography Belt Loop Hiking Belt Loop Marbles Belt Loop	Heritage Belt Loop Wildlife Conservation Belt Loop
Pack	Campfire Program / Hike	
Songs	America Oh, What Do You Do in the Summertime (245) "Give" Said the Little Stream (236)	
Other Activity	Leave No Trace (continued) World Conservation Fun For The Family – Courage	Family Assignment Fun For the Family – 3J, 5M, 5O

Wolf Plan for July

Achievement 2 – Your Flag	Home Assignment:
a) Give the Pledge of Allegiance to the flag of the United States of America. Tell what it means. b) Lead a flag ceremony in your den. c) Tell how to respect and take care of the U.S. flag. Show three ways to display it. d) Learn about the flag of your state or territory and how to display it. e) Learn how to raise a U.S. flag properly for an outdoor ceremony. f) Participate in an outdoor flag ceremony. g) With the help of another person, fold the flag.	Read pages 46 – 55. **Den Meeting:** Complete requirements 2a – 2g. **Pack Meeting:** Conduct a flag ceremony.

Elective 11 – Sing-Along

Read pages 162 – 165.

a) Learn and sing the first and last verses of "America."
b) Learn and sing the first verse of our national anthem.
c) Learn the words and sing three Cub Scout songs.
d) Learn the words and sing the first verse of three other songs, hymns, or prayers. Write the verse of one of the songs you learned.
e) Learn and sing a song that would be sung as a grace before meals.
f) Sing a song with your den at a pack meeting.

Elective 4 – Play a Game	Elective 18 – Outdoor Adventure
Read pages 128 – 131. a) Play Pie-tin Washer Toss. b) Play Marble Sharpshooter. c) Play Ring Toss. d) Play Beanbag Toss. e) Play a game of marbles. f) Play a wide-area or large group game with your den or pack.	Read pages 196 – 199. a) Help plan and hold a picnic. b) Help plan and run a family or den outing. c) Help plan and lay out a treasure hunt. d) Help plan and lay out an obstacle race. e) Help plan and lay out an adventure trail. f) Take part in two summertime pack events. g) Point out poisonous plants.

Marbles Belt Loop (Marbles is a lost art that Cub Scouts can help restore.)
1. Explain the rules of Ringer or another marble game to your leader or adult partner.
2. Spend at least 30 minutes practicing skills to play the game of Ringer or another marble game.
3. Participate in a game of marbles.

Bear Plan for July

Achievement 3 – What Makes America Special? f) Be a member of the color guard in a flag ceremony for your den or pack. g) Display the U.S. flag in your home or fly it on three national holidays. h) Learn how to raise and lower a U.S. flag properly for an outdoor ceremony. i) Participate in an outdoor flag ceremony.	**Home Assignment:** Read pages 34 – 41. Display U.S. flag at home or on three holidays. **Den Meeting:** Practice flag ceremony inside and outside. **Pack Meeting:** Conduct flag ceremony.
Achievement 12 – Family Outdoor Adventure Read pages 106 – 111. Complete three of the requirements. a) Go camping with your family. b) Go on a hike with your family. c) Have a picnic with your family. d) Attend an outdoor event with your family. e) Plan your outdoor family day.	**Elective 11 – Photography** Read pages 222 – 225. a) Learn how to use a camera. b) Take five pictures of the same subject in different kinds of light. c) Put your pictures in a scrapbook or framed. d) Take a picture in your house using available light.
Photography Belt Loop 1. Point out the major features of a camera to your den or family and explain the function of each part. Parts could include film, lens, shutter, power on and off, zoom, battery, flash, display panel, case, settings, etc. 2. Discuss with your den leader or adult partner, the benefits and contributions photography makes to modern life. Report what you learned to your den or family. 3. Using a camera, take at least 10 pictures of your family, pet, or scenery; show these to your den.	
Achievement 19 – Shavings and Chips a) Know the safety rules for handling a knife. b) Show that you know how to take care of and use a pocketknife. c) Make a carving with a pocketknife. d) Earn the Whittling Chip card.	**Home Assignment:** Read pages 146 – 151. **Den Meeting:** Complete all four requirements.
Wildlife Conservation Belt Loop 1. Explain what natural resources are and why it's important to protect and conserve them. 2. Make a poster that explains the food chain. Describe to your den what happens if the food chain becomes broken or damaged. 3. Learn about an endangered species. Make a report to your den that includes a picture, how the species came to be endangered, and what is being done to save it.	**Hiking Belt Loop** 1. Explain the hiking safety rules to your den leader or adult partner. Practice these rules while on a hike. 2. Demonstrate proper hiking attire and equipment. 3. Hike at least 30 minutes with your adult partner, family, or den.

Webelos Plan for July

Family Member (Community Group)	Home Assignment:
1. Tell what is meant by family, duty to family. 2. Make a chart showing the jobs you and other family members have at home. 3. Make a list of some things for which your family spends money. How can you help? 4. Plan and track your own budget for 30 days. 5. Take part in at least four family meetings and help make decisions. 6. Inspect your home and yard; list & fix hazard. Do two of these: 7. Prepare a family energy-saving plan. Explain what you did to carry it out. 8. Tell what your family does for fun. 9. Learn how to clean your home properly. 10. Take care of your clothes. 11. Plan the meals for your family for one week. 12. Earn the Heritages Academics belt loop. 13. Explain why garbage and trash must be disposed of properly.	Read pages 225 – 244. Complete 1 through 6 and two of the remaining seven requirements. **Den Meeting:** Review what was learned as a family member. **Heritage Belt Loop** 1. Talk with your family about your family heritage: its history, traditions, and culture. 2. Make a poster that shows the origins of your ancestors. Share it with your den. 3. Draw a family tree showing members of your family for three generations.
Citizen (Community) Required for Webelos	**Home Assignment:**
1. Character Connection for **Citizenship**. 2. Know President, Vice-President, state Governor, local head of government. 3. Explain flag history and etiquette. 4. How to respect the flag and when to fly it, etc. 5. Repeat and explain Pledge of Allegiance. 6. Tell how National Anthem was written. 7. Explain the rights and duties of a US citizen. 8. As a Webelos, earn the Citizenship belt loop. Do two of these: 9. Tell two things to help police / county sheriff. 10. Visit a community leader; learn their duties. 11. Write a short story about a former president. 12. Tell about a boy you think is a good citizen. 13. List three people who are good citizens. 14. Tell why we have and obey laws. 15. Tell why we have and pay for government. 16. List four ways the USA helps other nations. 17. Describe three organizations that help people.	Read pages 143 – 163. **Den Meeting:** Complete 1 through 8 then two 9 through 17. Progress and lessons learned are cover in the den meeting. Note: Citizen activity badge is covered twice each year to ensure that all boys have the opportunity to reach Webelos within the first six months. Note: Requirements for Outdoorsman, Naturalist, and Forester are outlined in June and August Guides.

August Core Value – Honesty

Faith in God	**Learning and Living the Gospel (6):** Tell a story from the Book of Mormon that teaches about faith in Jesus Christ. Share your testimony of the Savior. **(Cub Scout Religious Award)**	**13th Article of Faith**: We believe in being honest, true, chaste, benevolent, virtuous, and in doing good to all men; indeed, we may say that we follow the admonition of Paul—We believe all things, we hope all things, we have endured many things, and hope to be able to endure all things. If there is anything virtuous, lovely, or of good report or praiseworthy, we seek after these things. (Song: page 132)
Wolf	*Start a Collection (A6: a – c)* *Your Living World (A7: a – f)*	Birds (E13: a – f) Grow Something (E15: a – e)
Bear	*Sharing Your World with Wildlife (A5)* *Take Care of Your Planet (A6: 3 a – g)* *Water and Conservation (E15: a – e)*	Nature Craft (E12: a – d) Weather (E2: a – f)
Webelos / Arrow of Light	Naturalist Forester	
Sports / Academics	Collecting Belt Loop Wildlife Conservation Belt Loop	Golf Belt Loop Horseback Riding Belt Loop
Pack	Court of Honor / Pack Meeting	This is a very successful event. Include a slide show of the boy's summer camping / high adventure experience with pictures from the pack, EYOS, troop, team, and crew.
Songs	Oh, What Do You Do in the Summertime (245) All Things Bright and Beautiful (231)	My Heavenly Father Loves Me (228)
Other Activity	Complete Leave No Trace Fun For The Family – Honesty	Family Assignment Fun For the Family – 1E, 4R, 5Q

Wolf Plan for August

Achievement 6 – Start a Collection a) Character Connection for **Positive Attitude**. b) Make a collection. Start with 10 things. Put them together in a neat way. c) Explain your collection to another person.	**Home Assignment:** Read pages 70 – 73. Start a collection (see samples on page 72). **Den Meeting:** Share Collection at den and pack meeting.
Achievement 7 – Your Living World a) Character Connection for **Respect**. b) Land, air and water can get dirty. Discuss with your family ways this can happen. c) Find out how and what is recycled where you live. Find out what items you can recycle. d) Pick up litter in your neighborhood. Wear gloves to protect your hands. e) Find three stories that tell how people are protecting our world. Read and discuss. f) List three ways you can save energy, and do it.	**Home Assignment:** Read pages 74 – 77. Recycle, Reuse, and Conserve energy at home. **Den Meeting:** Discuss recycling and how Scouts can respect the environment and commit to recycling, reusing, and conserving energy. **Den Service Project:** Pick up litter at Park, Church, and School.
Elective 13 – Birds Read pages 174 – 177. a) Make a list of all the birds you saw in a week. b) Put out nesting material for birds. c) Read a book about birds. d) Point out 10 different kinds of birds. e) Feed wild birds and tell which birds you fed. f) Hang a birdhouse and tell which birds use it.	**Wildlife Conservation Belt Loop** 1. Explain what natural resources are and why they are protected and conserved. 2. Make a poster that shows and explains the food chain. Describe to your den what happens if the food chain becomes broken or damaged. 3. Learn about an endangered species. Make a report to your den that includes a picture, how the species came to be endangered, and what is being done to save it.

Cub Scout Leave No Trace Award (See page 102 in this guide.)
1. Discuss with an adult the importance of the Leave No Trace frontcountry guidelines.
2. On three separate outings, practice the frontcountry guidelines of Leave No Trace.
3. Boys complete the following for their rank:
   - Wolf – Requirement 7, Your Living World
   - Bear – Requirement 12, Family Outdoor Adventures
   - Webelos – Outdoorsman activity badge
4. Participate in a Leave No Trace-related service project.
5. Promise to practice the Leave No Trace frontcountry guidelines by signing the Cub Scout Leave No Trace Pledge.
6. Draw a poster to illustrate the Leave No Trace frontcountry guidelines and display it at a pack meeting.

Bear Plan for August

Achievement 5 – Sharing Your World with Wildlife a) Choose a bird or animal that you like and find out how it lives. Make a poster. b) Build or make a bird feeder or birdhouse. c) Explain a wildlife conservation officer. d) Visit one of the following: Zoo, Nature center, Aviary, Wildlife refuge, etc.	e) Name one animal that has become extinct in the last 100 years. **Home Assignment:** Read pages 50 – 55. **Den Meeting:** Complete four requirements.
Achievement 6 – Take Care of Your Plant a) Save 5 pounds of glass or aluminum. b) Plant a tree in your yard or community. c) Find out what happens to your trash. d) List all the ways water is used in your home. e) Discuss the kinds of energy your family uses.	f) Find out about your family's use of electricity. g) Take part in a neighborhood clean-up project. **Home Assignment:** Read pages 56 – 63. Complete three requirements.
Elective 2 – Weather Read pages 184 – 189. a) Learn how to read an outdoor thermometer. b) Build a weather vane. c) Make a rain gauge. d) Find out what a barometer is; how it works. e) Learn to identify three different kinds of clouds. Estimate their heights. f) Watch the weather forecast on TV every day for two weeks.	**Elective 12 – Nature Craft** Read pages 226 – 229. a) Make solar prints of three kinds of leaves. b) Make a display of eight different animal tracks with an eraser print. c) Collect, press, and label ten kinds of leaves. d) Build a waterscope and identify five types of water life. e) Collect and label eight kinds of plant seeds. f) Collect, mount, and label ten kinds of rocks or minerals. g) Collect, mount, and label five kinds of shells. h) Build and use a bird caller.
Elective 15 – Water and Soil Conservation Read pages 240 – 243. a) Dig a hole or find an excavation project and describe the different layers of soil you see and feel. (Do not enter an excavation area alone or without permission.) b) Explore three kinds of earth by conducting a soil experiment. c) Visit a burned-out forest or prairie area, or a slide area, with your den or your family. Talk to a soil and water conservation officer or forest ranger about how the area will be planted and cared for so that it will grow to be the way it was before the fire or slide. d) What is erosion? Find out the kinds of grasses, trees, or ground cover you should plant in your area to help limit erosion. e) As a den, visit a lake, stream, river, or ocean (whichever is nearest where you live). Plan and do a den project to help clean up this important source of water. Name four kinds of water pollution.	

Webelos Plan for August

Naturalist (Outdoors Group)	Forester (Outdoors Group)
Read pages 317 – 342. 1. Character Connection for **Respect**. Do five of the following: 2. Keep an insect zoo that you have collected. 3. Set up an aquarium or terrarium. 4. Visit a museum of natural history, nature center, or zoo. 5. Watch for birds in your area for one week. 6. Learn about the bird flyways closest to you. 7. Learn to identify poisonous plants and venomous reptiles found in your area. 8. Watch six wild animals in the wild. 9. Give examples of an ecosystem. 10. Identify a plant, bird, or wild animal that is found only in your area of the country. 11. Learn about aquatic ecosystems and wetlands. 12. Look around your neighborhood and identify how litter might be dangerous to wildlife. 13. Earn Wildlife Conservation belt loop. Webelos may still complete Outdoorsman, review requirements in previous guides.	Read pages 259 – 277. Do five of the following: 1. Make a map of the United States. Show the types of forests, names of trees, and where. 2. Draw a picture to show the plant and tree layers of a forest in your area. 3. Identify six forest trees common to the area where you live. Tell how wildlife and humans use them. 4. Identify six forest plants (other than trees) that are useful to wildlife. 5. Draw a picture showing: how water and minerals in the soil help a tree grow and how the tree uses sunlight to help it grow. 6. Make a poster showing a tree's growth rings or examine the growth rings of a tree stump. 7. Collect pieces of three kinds of wood used for building houses. 8. Plant 20 forest tree seedlings. 9. Describe both the benefits and the harm wildfires can cause in a forest ecosystem. 10. Draw your own urban forestry plan for adding trees to a street, yard, or park near your home.
Collecting Belt Loop 1. Begin a collection of at least 10 items that all have something in common. Label the items and title your collection. 2. Display your collection at a pack or den meeting. 3. Visit a show or museum that displays different collections.	**Golf Belt Loop** 1. Explain the rules of golf to your leader or adult partner. Explain the need for caution concerning golf clubs and golf balls. 2. Spend at least 30 minutes practicing golfing skills. 3. Participate in a round of golf (nine holes).

Horseback Riding Belt Loop
1. Explain five safety precautions for when you are near a horse.
2. With help from an experienced horse handler, demonstrate how to safely mount and ride a horse and then how to safely dismount the horse.
3. Go on a supervised horseback ride for at least 20 minutes. Wear an approved helmet (such as one approved for horseback riding by the ASTM, or American Society for Testing and Materials.)

LDS Guide to Scouting in the Primary

September Core Value – Cooperation

Faith in God	**Developing Talents (8):** List five things you can do to help around your home. Discuss the importance of obeying and honoring your parents and learning how to work.	**5th Article of Faith:** We believe that a man must be called of God, by prophecy, and by the laying on of hands by those who are in authority, to preach the Gospel and administer in the ordinances thereof. (Song: page 125)
Wolf	Feats of Skill (A1: a – e plus one f – l) *Keep Your Body Healthy (A3: a – c)*	Books, Books, Books (E6: a – c) Foot Power (E7: a – c) Sports (E20: a – o)
Bear	*Saving Well, Spending Well (A13: 4 a – g)* Games, Games, Games (A15: a – c) Sports, Sports, Sports (A23: a – e)	
Webelos / Arrow of Light	Sportsman *Scholar* **Outdoorsman** (Required for Arrow of Light)	Note: Ensure that each Webelos has completed Outdoorsman.
Sports / Academics	Kickball Belt Loop Flag Football Belt Loop Basketball Belt Loop Soccer Belt Loop	Reading and Writing Belt Loop Language Belt Loop (Webelos) Mathematics Belt Loop (Webelos) Chess Belt Loop (Webelos)
Pack	Games (Boys may share a collection that was started or added to over the summer.)	Plan fun games for the Cub Scouts and their siblings. Hold a parent orientation, kick-off and signup to assist with the pack meetings.
Songs	Beauty Everywhere (232) A Young Man Prepared (166) The Still Small Voice (106)	
Other Activity	Attend High School sports event Fun For The Family – Cooperation	Family Assignment Fun For the Family – 1A, 2F, 3D

Wolf Plan for September

Achievement 1 – Feats of Skill	Achievement 3 – Keeping Your Body Healthy
Read pages 38 – 45. a) Play catch with someone 10 steps away. b) Walk a line back and forth. c) Do a front roll. d) Do a back roll. e) Do a falling forward roll. Do one of the following: f) See how high you can jump. g) Do the elephant walk, frog leap, and crab walk. j) Using a basketball or playground ball, do a Chest pass, Bounce pass, Overhand Pass. k) Do a frog stand. l) Run or jog in place for 5 minutes.	a) Make a chart and keep track of your health habits for two weeks. b) Tell four ways to stop the spread of colds. c) Show what to do for a small cut on your finger. **Home Assignment:** Read pages 36 – 59. Complete 3a use a chart to track your health habits every day for two weeks. **Den Meeting:** Complete 3b and 3c; monitor chart.

Elective 20 – Sports

Read page 204 – 215.

BB Guns (215) and (206) Archery are completed only at Cub Scout day camp.

We will provide updated information on the sports we cover in den and pack meetings. The actual sports will depend on the interests and needs of all the boys in the pack. If a Webelos received the belt loop for a Sport or Academic while he was a Cub Scout, he is required to earn it again as a Webelos to use as a requirement for a Webelos activity badge. Depending on the ward budget upon completion of the requirements, he may or may not receive a second belt loop.

Elective 6 – Books, Books, Books

Read page 142 – 145.
a. Visit a bookstore or go to a public library with an adult. Find out how to get your own library card. Name four kinds of books that interest you (for example, history, science fiction, how-to-books).
b. Choose a book on a subject you like and read it. With an adult, discuss what you read and what you think about it.
c. Books are important. Show that you know how to take care of them. Open a new book the right way. Make a paper or plastic cover for it or another book.

Elective 7 – Foot Power

Read page 146 – 147.
a. Learn to walk on a pair of stilts.
b. Make a pair of "puddle jumpers" and walk with them.
c. Make a pair of "foot racers" and use them with a friend.

Bear Plan for September

Achievement 13 – Saving Well, Spending Well a. Go grocery shopping with a parent or other adult member of your family. b. Set up a savings account. c. Keep a record of how you spend money for two weeks. d. Pretend you are shopping for a car for your family. e. Discuss family finances with a parent or guardian. f. Play a board game with your family that involves the use of play money. g. With an adult, figure out how much it costs for each person in your home to eat one meal.	**Home Assignment:** Read pages 112 – 117. Complete four of the seven requirements. Note: Achievement 13 is part of the "Family" group of achievements. To earn your Bear rank you must complete four of the six achievements within the Family group. Bring the cars and comparative pricing to den meeting to discuss. Be prepared to explain which car you think will be the best choice for your family. Calculate the cost of a meal and determine your fast offering.
Achievement 15 – Games, Games, Games! a. Set up the equipment and play any two of these outdoor games with your family or friends: Backyard golf, Badminton, Croquet, Sidewalk shuffleboard, Kickball, Softball, Tetherball, Horseshoes, and Volleyball. b. Play two organized games with your den. c. Select a game that your den has never played. Explain the rules. Tell them how to play it, and then play it with them.	**Den Meeting:** Read pages 126 – 129. Complete two requirements. Den leader will provide information on the games that are played in the den and pack meeting. Note: Achievements 15 and 23 are part of the "Self" group. To earn the Bear rank you must earn four of the eleven achievements in the Self group.
Achievement 23 – Sports, Sports, Sports a. Learn the rules and how to play 3 team sports. b. Learn the rules on how to play two sports in which only one person is on each side. c. Take part in 1 team and 1 individual sport. d. Watch a sport on TV with a parent or some other adult member of your family. e. Attend a high school, college, or professional sporting event with your family or your den.	**Home Assignment:** Read pages 170 – 173. Complete requirements 23d and 23e. Check sports (individually and team) that you have played since your 9th birthday. **Den Meeting:** The actual sports covered will depend on the interests and needs of all the boys in the pack.

Webelos Plan for September

Sportsman (Physical Skills Group) 1. Show the signals used by officials in one of these sports: football, basketball, baseball, soccer, or hockey. 2. Explain what good sportsmanship means. 3. While you are a Webelos Scout, earn Cub Scout Sports belt loops for two individual sports: badminton, bicycling, bowling, fishing, golf, gymnastics, ice skating, marbles, physical fitness, roller skating, snow ski and board sports, swimming, table tennis, or tennis. 4. While you are a Webelos Scout, earn Cub Scout Sports belt loops for two team sports: baseball, basketball, soccer, softball, volleyball, flag football, or ultimate.	**Home Assignment:** Read pages 456 – 460. **Den Meeting:** a. Discuss requirements 1 and 2. b. The actual sports covered in the den meeting will depend on the interests and needs of all the boys in the pack. Webelos must earn the belt loop as a Webelos to count it towards an activity badge.
Scholar (Mental Skills Group) 1. Character Connection for **Positive Attitude**. 2. Have a good record in attendance, behavior, and grades at school. 3. Take an active part in a school activity/service. 4. Discuss with your teacher or principal the value of having an education. 5. Write some important things you can do now because of what you've learned in school. Earn the Language (6), Mathematics (7), and Chess (8) belt loops. 9. Trace through history the different kinds of schools. Tell how our present public school system grew out of these early schools. 10. Make a chart showing your school system. 11. Ask a parent and five other grown-ups these questions: What do you think are the best things about my school? What are its main problems? Tell what you think were the best answers and why. 12. List and explain some of the full-time positions in the field of education. 13. Help another student with schoolwork. Tell what you did to help.	**Home Assignment:** Read pages 392 – 400. Complete three of the requirements 2 – 8 including a discussion with your teacher or principal on the value of education. Complete three of the requirements 9 – 13 including asking adults the questions in requirement 11. **Den Meeting:** • Complete requirement 1. • Report on requirements 4 and 5 in den meeting. • Draw a chart for requirement 10. • Discuss answers to questions in requirement 11. • Discuss requirement 12.

Belt Loops for September

Basketball Belt Loop 1. Explain the rules of basketball to your leader or adult partner. 2. Spend at least 30 minutes practicing basketball skills. 3. Participate in a basketball game.	**Chess Belt Loop** 1. Identify the chess pieces and set up a chess board for play. 2. Demonstrate the moves of each chess piece to your den leader or adult partner. 3. Play a game of chess.
Flag Football Belt Loop 1. Explain or discuss the simple rules of flag football with your den. 2. Practice running, passing, and catching skills for at least 30 minutes. 3. Play a game of flag football.	**Kickball Belt Loop** 1. Explain the rules of kickball to your leader or adult partner. 2. Spend 30 minutes practicing the skills of kickball (pitching, kicking, base running, catching, throwing). This may be over two different practice periods. 3. Play a game of kickball.
Language Belt Loop 1. Talk with someone who grew up in a different country than you did. Find out what it was like and how it is different from your experience. 2. Learn 10 words that are in a different language than your own. 3. Play two games that originated in another country or culture.	**Mathematics Belt Loop** 1. Do five activities within your home or school that require the use of mathematics. Explain to your den how you used everyday math. 2. Keep track of the money you earn and spend for three weeks. 3. Measure five items using both metric and non metric measures. Find out about the history of the metric system of measurement.
Reading and Writing Belt Loop 1. Visit a library and get your own library card. Check out and return a book. 2. Write a letter or a short story. Read it to your den or family. 3. Keep a diary of your activities for one week. Read it to your den or family.	**Soccer Belt Loop** 1. Explain the rules of soccer to your leader or adult partner. 2. Spend at least 30 minutes practicing soccer skills. 3. Play a game of soccer.

October Core Value – Responsibility

Faith in God	**Learning and Living the Gospel (9):** Learn to sing "Choose the Right" (Hymns, no. 239). Explain what agency is and what it means to be responsible for your choices. Discuss how making good choices has helped you develop greater faith.	**2nd Article of Faith:** We believe that men will be punished for their own sins, and not for Adam's transgression. (Song: page 122)
Wolf	Know your Home & Community (A4) Be Safe at Home & On the Street (A9) Making Choices (A12: a – f) *Family Alert* (E16: a – c)	Bike rodeo is planned for the Spring. Visit Fire Station (Wolf A4: f) (alternates with Bear visit to Police Station.) Note: The pack rotates the visits to a police and fire station.
Bear	Law Enforcement a Big Job (A7: a – f) Be Ready! (A11: a – g)	Visit Police Station (Bear A7: b) (alternates with Wolf visit to Fir Station.)
Webelos / Arrow of Light	**Fitness** (Required for Webelos) **Readyman** (Required for Arrow of Light)	Webelos may choose to work on Fitness or Readyman requirements, if two-deep leadership is available for both Wolf/Bear field trip and Webelos activity.
Sports / Academics	Physical Fitness Belt Loop Roller Skating Belt Loop	Softball Belt Loop Ultimate Belt Loop Pet Care Belt Loop
Pack	Be Prepared – Guest speaker (Ward member who is a policeman, fireman, or works in public service field.) Prepare a Family Escape route (Bear A11: e) Fire Safety Month – Boys may participate in special community service project.	
Songs	Keep the Commandments (146) Choose the Right (Hymn 239)	
Other Activity	Primary Sacrament Program Fun For The Family – Responsibility	Family Assignment Fun For the Family – 4L, 5E, 2K, 3G

Wolf Plan for October

Achievement 4 – Know Your Home and Community	Home Assignment:
a) Make a list of phone numbers you need in case of an emergency. Put a copy of this list by each phone or in a central place in your home. b) Tell what to do if someone comes to the door and wants to come in. c) Tell what to do if someone calls on the phone. d) When you and your family leave home, remember to checklist. e) Talk with your family members. Make and use job chart for one month. f) Visit an important place in your community, such as a historic or government location.	Read pages 60 – 63. Complete 4a – 4e; discuss in a den meeting then completed at home. Phone lists and checklist are in Wolf Handbook. Create a job chart to list family member's assignments. A job chart is also requirement 3M in "Fun For The Family". **Den Meeting:** Alternate visiting Police and Fire Station. **Pack Meeting:** Alternate inviting a policeman, fireman, paramedics. Be prepared.
Achievement 9 – Be Safe at Home and on the Street a) Character Connection for **Responsibility.** b) Check your home for hazards and know how to make your home safe. c) Check your home for danger from fire. d) Practice good rules of street and road safety. e) Know the rules of bike safety.	**Home Assignment:** Read pages 82 – 87. Complete 9a – 9e at home. **Den Meeting:** Discuss or review 9a – 9e. Note: Bike rodeo is held in the spring.
Achievement 12 – Making Choices Read pages 100 – 106. a) Character Connection for **Courage.** b) Complete 12b – 12f. Note: Achievement 12 is covered in the Spring.	**Den Meeting:** Complete 12a – 12f. **Pack Meeting:** Sing Song – "Choose the Right".
Elective 16 – Family Alert Read page 188. a) Talk with your family about what you will do in an emergency. b) In case of a bad storm or flood, know where you can get safe food and water in your home. Tell how to purify water. Show one way. Know where and how to shut off water, electricity, gas, or oil. c) Make a list of your first aid supplies, or make a first aid kit. Know where the first aid things are kept.	

LDS Guide to Scouting in the Primary

Bear Plan for October

Achievement 7 – Law Enforcement is a Big Job Do all six requirements: a) Practice one way police gather evidence: by taking fingerprints, or taking shoeprints, or taking tire track casts. b) Visit your local sheriff's office or police station or talk with a law enforcement officer visiting your den or pack to discuss crime prevention. c) Help with crime prevention for your home. d) Be sure you know where to get help in your neighborhood. e) Learn the phone numbers to use in an emergency and post them by each phone in your home. f) Know what you can do to help law enforcement.	**Home Assignment:** Read pages 64 – 71. Complete the following: c) List how to protect your home. d) List four names, addresses, and phones numbers of neighbors who can help you. e) Learn emergency phone numbers and post them by the phones. Include; Police, Fire, Medical, Poison Control Center, other. **Den Meeting:** a) Fingerprinting. b) Alternate inviting a policeman, fireman, paramedics. f) Discuss what you can do to help law enforcement.
Achievement 11 – Be Ready! a) Tell what to do in case of an accident in the home when a family member needs help. b) Tell what to do in case of a water accident. c) Tell what to do in case of a school bus accident. d) Tell what to do in case of a car accident. e) With your family, plan escape routes from your home and have a practice drill. f) Have a health checkup by a physician (optional). g) Character Connection for **Courage**.	**Home Assignment:** Read pages 96 – 105. After den meeting, share what your Scout has learned with the entire family. Complete 11e: practice an escape route. **Den Meeting:** Discuss and reenact accidents using right and wrong ways to react in each situation. Complete 11a, 11b, 11c, 11d, and 11g. **Pack Meeting:** Gathering activity for pack meeting will be 11e.
Fitness Belt Loop 1. Give a short report to your den or family on the dangers of drugs and alcohol. 2. Practice finding your pulse and counting your heart beats per minute. Determine your target heart rate. 3. Practice five physical fitness skills regularly. Improve performance in each skill over a month. Skills could include pull-ups, curl-ups, the standing long jump, the 50-yard dash, and the softball throw.	**Home Assignment:** Complete physical fitness chart to use to track physical fitness skills over time. The Physical Fitness belt loop and pin are an alternative if the den has already completed Achievements 7 and 11.

Webelos Plan for October

Fitness (Physical Group) Required for Webelos 1. Character Connection for **Health and Fitness**. Explain what good sportsmanship means. 2. With your parents, complete a safety notebook described in "How to Protect Your Child from Child Abuse." 3. With parents plan a week of meals. 4. Track meals and snacks for one week. 5. Discuss harmful effects of tobacco with family. 6. Discuss the effects of alcohol with your family. 7. Discuss harmful effects of drugs with family. 8. Read BSA booklet "Choose to Refuse" and discuss with an adult.	**Home Assignment:** Read pages 245 – 258. Complete #1 and six of the remaining seven requirements. Fitness is the responsibility of the Cub Scout and his parents. Progress and lessons learned are covered in the den meeting. **Den Meeting:** Review what was learned Fitness 1 – 8. Note: This activity badge is covered twice each year to ensure all boys have the opportunity to reach Webelos within their first six months.
Readyman (Community Group) Required for Arrow of Light 1. Character Connection for **Courage**. 2. Explain what first aid is. Tell what you should do after an accident. 3. Explain how you can get help quickly if there is an emergency in your home. Make a Help List of people or agencies that can help you if you need it. Post it near a phone. 4. Demonstrate the Heimlich maneuver. 5. Show what to do for these "hurry cases". 6. Show how to treat shock. 7. Show first aid for common situations. 8. Discuss safe swim and the buddy system. Do two of the following: 9. Explain six safety rules for riding a bicycle. 10. Discuss wearing sports safety equipment. 11. Make a home fire escape plan for your family. 12. Explain how to use each item in a first aid kit. 13. Tell where accidents are most likely to happen inside and around your home. 14. Explain six car safety rules. 15. Attend a first aid demonstration at a Boy Scout troop meeting, a Red Cross center, etc.	**Home Assignment:** Read pages 365 – 390. Readyman is completed in den meetings and requires several den meetings to finish. It is important to also discuss what is covered in the den meetings with family members so the entire family is prepared if an accident occurs. **Den Meeting:** Complete requirement 1 – 8. Select at least two of the remaining requirements to complete. **Pack Meeting:** Requirement 11 is completed in the pack meeting.

Belt Loops for October

Fitness Belt Loop	Roller Skating Belt Loop
1. Give a short report to your den or family on the dangers of drugs and alcohol. 2. Practice finding your pulse and counting your heart beats per minute. Determine your target heart rate. 3. Practice five physical fitness skills regularly. Improve performance in each skill over a month. Skills could include pull-ups, curl-ups, the standing long jump, the 50-yard dash, and the softball throw.	1. Explain ways to protect you while roller skating or inline skating, and the need for proper safety equipment. 2. Spend at least 30 minutes practicing the skills of roller skating or inline skating. 3. Go skating with a family member or den for at least three hours. Chart your time.
Softball Belt Loop 1. Explain the rules of softball to your leader or adult partner. 2. Spend at least 30 minutes practicing softball skills. 3. Participate in a softball game.	**Ultimate Belt Loop** 1. Explain the rules of ultimate to your leader or adult partner. 2. Spend at least 30 minutes practicing ultimate skills. 3. Participate in an ultimate game.

November Core Value – Citizenship

Faith in God	**Serving Others (8):** Read the twelfth article of faith. Discuss what it means to be a good citizen and how your actions can affect others.	**12th Article of Faith:** We believe in being subject to kings, presidents, rulers, and magistrates, in obeying, honoring, and sustaining the law. (Song: page 131)
Wolf	Your Flag (A2: a – g) *Your Living World (A7: a – f)* Duty to God (A11: a – d)	American Indian Signs (E1: a) American Indian Lore (E10: a – f)
Bear	Ways We Worship (A1) What Makes America Special (A3)	American Indian Life (E:24 a – b) Prepare Tall Tales for pack meeting.
Webelos / Arrow of Light	**Citizen** (Required for Webelos) Showman	Puppetry, drama, or music performance at ward Christmas program or December pack meeting.
Sports / Academics	Language and Culture Belt Loop Citizenship Belt Loop and Pin	
Pack	Speaker – Public official speak about election process and public service	An American Indian Packet is available to use over the Thanksgiving Holiday.
Songs	My Flag, My Flag (226) I'm Trying To Be Like Jesus (78) Book of Mormon Stories (118)	
Other Activity	Fun For The Family – Citizenship	Family Assignment Fun For the Family – 2A, 3C, 4G, 4Q

Wolf Plan for November

Achievement 2 – Your Flag a) Give the Pledge of Allegiance to the flag of the United States of America. Tell what it means. b) Lead a flag ceremony in your den. c) Tell how to respect and take care of the U.S. flag. Show three ways to display it. d) Learn about the flag of your state or territory and how to display it. e) Learn how to raise a U.S. flag properly for an outdoor ceremony.	f) Participate in an outdoor flag ceremony. g) With another person, fold the flag. **Home Assignment:** Read pages 46 – 55. **Den Meeting:** Complete requirements 2a – 2g. **Pack Meeting:** Conduct a flag ceremony.
Achievement 7 – Your Living World a) Character Connection for **Respect**. b) Land, air and water can get dirty. Discuss with your family ways this can happen. c) Find out how and what is recycled where you live. Find out what items you can recycle. d) Pick up litter in your neighborhood. Wear gloves to protect your hands. e) Find three stories that tell how people are protecting our world. Read and discuss. f) List three ways you can save energy, and do it.	**Home Assignment:** Read pages 74 – 77. Recycle, reuse, and conserve energy at home. **Den Meeting:** Discuss recycling and how Scouts can respect the environment and commit to recycling, reusing, and conserving energy. **Den Service Project:** Pick up litter at church and school.
Achievement 11 – Duty to God a) Character Connection for **Faith**. b) Talk with your family about what they believe. c) Give two ideas on how you can practice or demonstrate your religious beliefs. d) Find out how you can help your church.	**Home Assignment:** Read pages 94 – 99. Complete 11b and 11c. **Den Meeting:** Complete 11a – Discuss pilgrims and pioneers.
Elective 1 – It's a Secret Read Pages 114 – 117. d) Use 12 American Indian signs to tell a story. **Elective 11 – American Indian Lore** Read Pages 154 – 161. (Activities can be shared at pack meeting.) a) Read a book or tell a story about American Indians, past or present. b) Make a musical instrument American Indians used. c) Make traditional American Indian clothing. d) Make a traditional item or instrument that American Indians used to make their lives easier. e) Make a model of a traditional American Indian house. f) Learn 12 American Indian word pictures and write a story with them.	

Bear Plan for November

Achievement 1 – Ways We Worship a) Character Connection for **Faith**. b) Make a list of things you can do this week to practice your religion as you are taught in your home and church. Check them off your list as you complete them.	**Home Assignment**: Read pages 26 – 29. Complete 1a and make a list of ways you practice your religion at home, at school, at play, and at Scouts. **Den Meeting**: Review lists and discuss den rules.
Achievement 3 – What Makes America Special? a) Write or tell what makes America special. b) Find out about two famous Americans. Tell the things they did to improve our way of life. c) Find out something about the old homes near where you live. Go and see two of them. d) Find out where places of historical interest are located in or near your town or city. Go and visit one of them with your family or den. e) Choose a state. Name its state bird, tree, flag, flower, and the date admitted to the Union. f) Be a member of the color guard in a flag ceremony for your den or pack. g) Display the U.S. flag in your home or fly it on three national holidays. h) Learn how to raise and lower a U.S. flag properly for an outdoor ceremony. i) Participate in an outdoor flag ceremony. j) Character Connection for **Citizenship**.	**Home Assignment**: Read pages 34 – 41. Complete 3a and 3j plus two other requirements. Display U.S. flag at home or on three holidays. **Den Meeting**: Discuss citizenship and what makes America special. Practice flag ceremony inside and outside. **Pack Meeting**: Conduct flag ceremony.
Achievement 4 – Tall Tales a) Tell in your own words what folklore is. List some folklore stories, folk songs, or historical legends from your own state or part of the country. Play the Folklore Match Game in the handbook. b) Name at least five stories about American folklore. Point out on a United States map where they happened. c) Read two folklore stories and tell your favorite one to your den.	**Home Assignment**: Read pages 42 – 49. **Den Meeting**: Complete all three requirements.
Elective 24 – American Indian Life a) Learn about Indians who lived where you live. b) Play two Indian games. c) Make shelter model for Indians who lived here.	**Home Assignment**: Read pages 272 – 275.

Webelos Plan for November

Citizen (Community) Required for Webelos 1. Character Connection for **Citizenship**. 2. Know President, Vice-President, state Governor, local head of government. 3. Explain flag history and etiquette. 4. How to respect the flag and when to fly it, etc. 5. Repeat and explain Pledge of Allegiance. 6. Tell how National Anthem was written. 7. Explain the rights and duties of a US citizen. 8. As a Webelos, earn the Citizenship belt loop. Do two of these: 9. Tell two things to help police / county sheriff. 10. Visit a community leader; learn their duties. 11. Write a short story about a former president. 12. Tell about a boy you think is a good citizen. 13. List three people who are good citizens. 14. Tell why we have and obey laws. Which have you obeyed this week? 15. Tell why we have and pay for government. 16. List four ways the USA helps other nations. 17. Describe three organizations that help people.	**Home Assignment:** Read pages 143 – 163. **Den Meeting:** Complete 1 through 8 then two 9 through 17. Progress and lessons learned are covered in the den meeting. See requirements below for belt loop. **Note**: This activity badge is covered twice each year to ensure all boys have the opportunity to reach Webelos within the first six months.
Showman (Mental Group) **Requirements are listed on pages 430 – 432.** • Complete six activities of your choice; these can be from puppetry, music, or drama. • And, do one additional requirement from each area: Puppetry, Music, and Drama. Showman requires the completion of a total of nine requirements.	**Home Assignment:** Read pages 429 – 453. This activity badge is customized for each boy. **Pack Meting**: Plan to perform at the December pack meeting.
Citizenship Belt Loop 1. Develop a list of jobs you can do around the home. Chart your progress for one week. 2. Make a poster showing things that you can do to be a good citizen. 3. Participate in a family, den, or school service project. **Note**: The Citizenship belt loop is required for the Citizen activity badge.	**Language and Culture Belt Loop** 1. Talk with someone who grew up in a different country than you did. Find out what it was like and how it is different from your experience. 2. Learn 10 words that are in a different language than your own. 3. Play two games that originated in another country or culture.

December Core Value – Respect

Faith in God	**Serving Other (2):** Write a letter to a teacher, your parents, or your grandparents telling them what you appreciate and respect about them.	**11th Article of Faith:** We claim the privilege of worshiping Almighty God according to the dictates of our own conscience, and allow all men the same privilege, let them worship how, where, or what they may. (Song: page 130)
Wolf	*Family Fun (A10: a plus 2 b – g)* Tools for Fixing and Building (A5: a – e) Make it Yourself (E3: a – e)	Pets (E14: a – d) Be an Actor (E2: a – e)
Bear	Tall Tales (A4: a – c) Family Fun (A10: a – b) Sawdust and Nails (A20: a – c)	Cub Scout Band (E8: a – d)
Webelos / Arrow of Light	*Family Member* Handyman Showman	Complete Showman with a performance at ward Christmas Party or pack meeting.
Sports / Academics	Heritages Belt Loop Good Manners Belt Loop	Pet Care Belt Loop
Pack	Service Project Den Skits (America / Indian Lore / Tall Tales)	
Songs	Christmas Songs Book of Mormon Stories (118) Pioneer Children Were Quick to Obey (215)	
Other Activity	Primary Christmas Program Fun For The Family – Respect	Family Assignment Fun For the Family – 1G, 3I, 4E

Wolf Plan for December

Achievement 10 – Family Fun **Home Assignment:** Read pages 88 – 93. Complete 10a and two 10b through 10g. a) Character Connection for **Cooperation**. b) Make a game and play it with your family. c) Plan a walk. Go to a park or a wooded area, or visit a zoo or museum with your family. d) Read a book or Boys' Life magazine with your family. Take turns reading aloud. e) Decide with Akela, what you will watch on television or listen to on the radio. f) Attend a concert, a play, or other live program with your family. g) Have a family board game night at home with members of your family.	**Elective 14 – Pets** a) Take care of a pet. b) Know what to do when you meet a strange dog. c) Read a book about a pet and tell about it at a den meeting. d) Tell what is meant by rabid. Name some animals that can have rabies. Tell what you should do if you see a dog or wild animal that is behaving strangely. e) Tell what you should do if you find a dead animal. **Home Assignment:** Read pages 178 – 183. Complete E14a.
Achievement 5 – Tools for Fixing and Building a) Point out and name seven tools. Do this at home, or go to a hardware store with an adult. Tell what each tool does. b) Show how to use pliers. c) Identify a Philips head and a standard screw. Then use the right tool to drive and then remove one from a board. d) Show how to use a hammer. e) Make a birdhouse, a set of bookends, or something else useful.	**Home Assignment:** Read pages 64 – 69. **Den Meeting:** Make a useful item for the home and give it to parents or grandparents as a present.
Elective 3 – Make It Yourself Read pages 124 – 127. a) Make something useful for your home or school. Start with a recipe card holder. b) Use the ruler on this page (125) to see how far you can stretch your hand. c) Make and use a bench fork. d) Make a door stop. e) Or make something else.	**Elective 2 – Be an Actor** Read pages 118 – 123. a) Help to plan and put on a skit with costumes. b) Make some scenery for a skit. c) Make sound effects for a skit. d) Be the announcer for a skit. e) Make a paper sack mask for a skit.

Bear Plan for December

Achievement 10 – Family Fun a) Go on a day trip or evening out with members of your family. b) Have a family fun night at home.	**Home Assignment:** Read pages 90 – 95. Complete both requirements.
Achievement 4 – Tall Tales Read pages 42 – 49. a) Tell in your own words what folklore is. List some folklore stories, folk songs, or historical legends from your own state or part of the country. Play the Folklore Match Game in the handbook. b) Name at least five stories about American folklore. Point out on a United States map where they happened. c) Read two folklore stories and tell your favorite one to your den.	**Elective 8 – Cub Scout Band** Read pages 210 – 113. a) Make and play a homemade musical instrument, pages 211 – 212. b) Learn to play two familiar tunes on any musical instrument. c) Play in a den band using homemade or regular musical instruments. Play at a pack meeting. d) Play two tunes on any recognized instrument.
Achievement 20 – Sawdust and Nails a) Show how to use and take care of four of these tools: Hammer, Hand saw, Hand drill, C-clamp, Wood plane, Pliers, Crescent wrench, Screwdriver, Bench vise, Coping saw, Drill bit. b) Build your own tool box. c) Use at least two tools listed in requirement (a) to fix something.	**Home Assignment:** Read pages 152 – 155. Complete 20c at home. **Den Meeting:** Complete 20a and 20b plus make an object for family.
Good Manners Belt Loop 1. Make a poster that lists five good manners that you want to practice. Share your poster with your den or family. 2. Introduce two people correctly and politely. Be sure that one of them is an adult. 3. Write a thank-you note to someone who has given you something or done something nice for you.	**Pet Care Belt Loop** 1. Care for your pet for two weeks. Make a list of the tasks that you did to take care of your pet. 2. Read a book, explore the Internet (with your parent's or partner's permission), or acquire a pamphlet about your pet. List three interesting facts that you learned about your pet. 3. Make a poster about your pet. Share your poster with your den, pack, or family.

Webelos Plan for December

Family Member (Community Group)	Home Assignment:
1. Tell what is meant by family, duty to family. 2. Make a chart showing the jobs you and other family members have at home. 3. Make a list of some things for which your family spends money. How can you help? 4. Plan and track your own budget for 30 days. 5. Take part in at least four family meetings and help make decisions. 6. With an adult inspect your home and surroundings. Make a list and correct a hazard. Do two of the following: 7. Prepare a family energy-saving plan. Explain what you did to carry it out. 8. Tell what your family does for fun. 9. Learn how to clean your home properly. 10. Take care of your clothes. 11. Plan the meals for your family for one week. 12. Earn the Heritages Academics belt loop. 13. Explain why garbage and trash must be disposed of properly.	Read pages 225 – 244. Complete 1 through 6 and two of the remaining seven requirements. **Den Meeting:** Review what was learned as a Family Member. **Heritage Belt Loop** 1. Talk with your family about your family heritage: its history, traditions, and culture. 2. Make a poster that shows the origins of your ancestors. Share it with your den. 3. Draw a family tree showing members of your family for three generations.
Handyman (Technology Group) 1. Character Connection for **Responsibility**. Do six of the following: 2. With adult supervision, wash a car. 3. Help an adult change a tire on a car. 4. Replace a bulb in the taillight, turn signal, etc. 5. Check the oil level and tire pressure on a car. 6. Repair to a bicycle, chain, seat or handlebars. 7. Properly lubricate the chain and crank on bike. 8. Properly inflate the tires on a bicycle. 9. Change the wheels on a skateboard. 10. Replace a light bulb in a fixture or lamp. 11. Arrange a storage area for household cleaners. 12. Build a sawhorse or stool to be used in home. 13. Help take care of the lawn. 14. Arrange a storage area for hand tools. 15. Clean and properly store hand tools. 16. Label hand tools or lawn and garden tools. 17. Put together a toolbox for common repairs.	**Home Assignment:** Read pages 299 – 316. **Den Meeting:** Complete six of the sixteen requirements.

LDS Guide to Scouting in the Primary

Eleven-Year-Old-Scouts

Scouting for Eleven-Year-Olds

An EYOS (eleven-year-old Scout) patrol provides a boy with a group of boys his own age in which he can earn awards and recognition. In the EYOS patrol, he gains a sense of personal achievement for the new skills he learns. The EYOS organization and purpose are similar to the Cub Scout program.

Although under the Primary, the EYOS is a patrol in the ward's Boy Scout troop. The EYOS leader is an Assistant Scoutmaster and participates in the troop committee meeting. A woman can be the EYOS leader but she does not participate in overnight activities. If an EYOS leader is not called, the Primary teacher or member of the Primary presidency over Scouting assists in working with the boys on Scouting and Faith in God activities.

It is recommended that the EYOS meet separately from the Boy Scout troop most of the time. They are still part of Primary and the Primary president is responsible for the program. The Primary president attends basic training to have a better understanding of the role of Scouting in the Church

Preparing For the Priesthood (Faith in God Award)

Boys continue to work on Faith in God by completing the following activities while they are eleven.

- Learn about the restoration of the Aaronic Priesthood (see D&C 13, 107:20, and Joseph Smith—History 1:68–73).
- Read D&C 20:57–60 and Aaronic Priesthood: Fulfilling Our Duty to God [Deacon], Page 7. Discuss with a parent or leader the purposes of the Aaronic Priesthood and what it means to do your duty to God.
- Talk with the deacon's quorum Presidency about the role of the deacons quorum. Write in your journal how you can serve the Lord as a member of a deacon's quorum.
- Read D&C 88:77–80, 118 and D&C 130:19. Discuss with a parent or Primary leader how important a good education is and how it can help strengthen you as a priesthood holder in your home and family and in the Church.
- Read "The Family: A Proclamation to the World." Make a list of things you can do to help strengthen your family and make a happy home. Share the list with your parents or Primary leader.

Teaching 11-year-old Scouts is a great responsibility. They are out of Cub Scouts and excited to be a Boy Scout and are teachable at this age.

"Scouting prepares eleven-year-old boys to receive the Aaronic Priesthood and transition in to the deacons quorum and Young Men program. Scouting can help them increase in confidence, testimony, brotherhood, and understanding of Aaronic Priesthood duties. The eleven-year-old boy will need to establish good relationships with his peers, the deacons quorum presidency, and his leaders." (Scouting Handbook, page 3)

The EYOS Program

The Church believes that there is a significant difference in the characteristics and needs of eleven-year-old boys as compared to eight to ten and twelve to thirteen-year-old boys. The eleventh year is the transition year between boys and young men, thus the Scouting Handbook, pages 3 – 4, identifies the way that the Scouting program is implemented for eleven year-old Scouts.

It is during this period of a boy's life that he experiences puberty, or the transition from boyhood to manhood. With some boys the transition happens quickly. With others it may take a while. Lord Baden-Powell once said: *"The Scoutmaster . . . must realize the needs, outlooks and desires of the different ages of the boy's life. He must deal with the individual boy rather than the mass."*

The age, physical size, and developmental stage of boys often do not coincide. Despite the well-meaning but mistaken belief of some adults, children and youth are not small adults. They understand things differently and act on things for different reasons than adults do. When we treat children and youth as adults, they become frustrated because we do not appear to listen to or understand them.

By understanding the characteristics and needs of the boys in the troop, leaders have more success in providing boys with activities they see as fun to participate in, and adults are able to figure out ways to use the activities as vehicles for teaching skills and values to the boys.

Essential Books for the EYOS Leader

To insure a quality program the following resources are valuable references for the EYOS leader.

- Boy Scout Handbook
- Scoutmaster Handbook
- The Guide to Safe Scouting
- LDS Scouting Handbook
- Scouting & The Church of Jesus Christ of Latter-day Saints
- Troop Program Resource Book

Keys to a Successful Program

- **Maintain accurate records for each boy.** There are both paper and electronic record keeping programs. It is very important to fill out the record chart for each boy and monitor his progress so the leader and parents can see at a glance where each boy is in advancement.

- **Know the advancement requirements.** Become familiar with the requirements up through the First Class Scout. Boys can work on the requirements in any order, but they must complete all requirements for Tenderfoot to receive that award. Tenderfoot must be earned before the boy receives the Second Class rank then he can receive the First Class rank. He may receive all three badges at the same time.

LDS Guide to Scouting in the Primary

- **Teach the boys to lead.** EYOS leaders should be aware of the patrol positions necessary to operate the patrol. The Church does not hold elections but the bishopric appoints boys so they all have opportunities to have leadership experiences.

"In consultation with the ward Primary presidency and the eleven-year-old Scouts leader, the bishopric appoints one of the boys to serve as the patrol leader. He may meet occasionally with the older troop leaders when they plan events that will include the eleven-year old patrol. The patrol leader should, with adult leader assistance, choose assistant patrol leaders and assign other duties in the patrol as needed." (Scouting Handbook, page 4)

  - The Patrol Leader has the responsibility for the patrol's activities and represents the patrol as a member of the patrol leaders' council.
  - The Assistant Patrol Leader helps the patrol leader and acts as the patrol leader when the patrol leader is not present.
  - Scribe is the patrol's secretary. He attends meetings of the patrol leaders and keeps a log of what was discussed. He records troop attendance and maintains troop advancement records.
  - Quartermaster is the supply and equipment boss. He keeps an inventory of troop equipment and sees that it is in good condition.

- **Select a Troop Guide.** With the assistance of the Scoutmaster, Young Men presidency, and Primary president choose a troop guide (usually a scout who has achieved First Class).

- **Encourage Scouting Spirit.** Let each patrol under the direction of the patrol leader choose a patrol name, yell, song, flag, and patch.

- **Hold a Patrol Leader Council (PLC).** Meetings are scheduled regularly with the EYOS leader, troop guide, patrol leader(s), and scribe(s). The patrol leader is in charge of this meeting and is guided by the EYOS leader. In the PLC meetings, patrol meetings and activities are planned.

- **Organize the calendar.** Start by assessing each boy's requirements to advance to First Class before his 12th birthday.
  - Boys should complete the physical fitness requirements as soon as possible, because this can hold them back from receiving the Tenderfoot rank.
  - Review the patrol leader council's calendar.
  - Plan the patrol meetings for the next month, three months, and year.

The EYOS Orientation

When a boy turns eleven years old, the EYOS leader, troop guide, and patrol leader provide the boy and his parent(s) with an overview of the EYOS program and the patrol's expectations. Prior to the meeting, the boy will need a Boy Scout Handbook, rope to tie a square knot, and the following assignments for parents and boys to read in the Boy Scout Handbook:

- Boy – Pages 1 – 15 "The Adventure Begins"
- Parents – "How to Protect Your Child from Child Abuse: A Parent's Guide"

The orientation includes:

- Requirements for joining the troop (boy demonstrates the Square Knot).
- Registration forms for the boy and parents.
- The Scout Uniform and Insignias.
- The Scouting activities and calendar of events.
- The Advancement plan to reach First Class by twelve and Eagle by sixteen.
- Scouting costs and fund raising expectations.
- The Faith in God requirements for eleven-year-old boys

The Orientation Packet Materials:

- Boy Scout Registration Form
- Health Record / Medical Form for the Boy Scout
- Annual calendar of events with dates
- Scout uniform options and costs
- Troop Numbers and patrol Patch
- Boy's position description and corresponding patch
- Uniform guide to use when sewing patches onto uniform
- Individual Scout Record
- First Year Tracking Form
- Adult Volunteer Registration Forms
- Parent Survey that includes hobbies and interests

The boy should already have a copy of the Boy Scout Handbook that he should bring it to every patrol meeting.

Trail to First Class

With good attendance at patrol meetings and activities, it is a very realistic goal to attain the rank of First Class by the time the boy turns twelve years old. Remember: Like Cub Scouts Wolf, Bear and Webelos, the ranks of Tenderfoot, Second Class, and First Class are awarded in order, however unlike Cub Scouts; EYOS may work on the requirements for the three ranks simultaneously.

Scouts may also work on merit badges. (EYOS do not focus on merit badges but on the many requirements for the first three ranks.) To complete the requirements for Star, Life, and Eagle the Scout must pass off both required and elected merit badges that explore areas such as canoeing, swimming, camping, astronomy, citizenship, etc. Counselors are available to assist the boys in completing the requirements and teach them the skills outlined for the merit badge.

Key points in attaining the rank of First Class:

- Scouts participate in ten patrol/troop activities (five for Second Class) after joining the EYOS patrol in the troop, excluding troop meetings. It is important to participate in as many activities as possible; many outdoor requirements cannot be done at the troop meetings. Also, the "ten activities" requirement is almost always the hardest and the last completed for First Class.
- Three of these activities need to include camping overnight in a tent (one for each rank); it is important to take advantage of all the camping trips. Fathers may plan to go with their sons on camping trips but it is not required. Boys may not sleep in a tent with an adult who is not their parent. EYOS may camp with the Boy Scout troop.
- Swimming and Orienteering requirements are hard to pass off without the patrol and it is hard for the patrol to repeat; boys are encouraged to attend theses when they are scheduled.
- Cooking requirements include menu planning and food procurement, as well as functioning as the head-cook. Scouts and parents are encouraged to sign-up for campouts of their choice with the troop committee.
- Community service is required for Second Class rank advancement. Participation in Eagle projects with the older scouts and other troop service activities can fulfill this requirement.
- Plant and animal identification may be difficult in the winter. Scouts are encouraged to complete these requirements on the fall or spring nature hike.
- Good attendance and attention at patrol meetings and activities will ensure that each Scout masters the skills needed to earn the rank of First Class by his birthday.

The advancement program is designed to provide the Boy Scout with a chance to achieve the aims of Scouting. As a Scout advances, he is measured and grows in confidence and self-reliance. He demonstrates that he is living the Scout Oath (Promise) and Law in his daily life. He learns leadership by serving his patrol in a position of responsibility and he serves his community through service projects and doing good turns daily. After a Scoutmaster's conference and a board of review, the boy is awarded the ranks at the troop's quarterly court of honor.

The Troop Guide

Similar to a den chief in the Cub Scout pack, a troop guide can be a mentor to the younger Scouts and an assistant to the EYOS leaders. A troop guide is an older Scout (Deacon, Teacher or Priest) who has attained the rank of at least First Class. It is a leadership position for Star, Life, and Eagle ranks. They assist in the program and teach the boys the skills. Boys love to learn from older boys and look up to them as role models. They see that someone else has actually learned and been successful. The troop guide also has a built-in ability to relate to the younger boys on their level.

Job Description: The troop guide works with the new Scouts. He helps them earn their Tenderfoot, Second Class, and First Class ranks within their first year. He reports to the eleven-year-old Scout leader.

Troop Guide Duties:

- Introduces the new Scouts to troop operations.
- Guides new Scouts through early Scouting activities.
- Shields the new Scouts from harassment by older Scouts.
- Helps new Scouts earn First Class rank in their first year.
- Teaches basic Scout skills.
- Coaches the patrol leader of the EYOS patrol on his duties.
- Works with the patrol leader at patrol leaders' council meetings.
- Attends patrol leaders' council meetings with the patrol leader.
- Assists the EYOS leader with training eleven-year-old Scouts.
- Counsels individual Scouts on Scout challenges.
- Sets a good example.
- Enthusiastically wears the Scout uniform correctly.
- Lives by the Scout Oath and Law.
- Shows Scout spirit.

The BSA "requirement approval process" consists of a skill instructional period followed by a testing period that should be performed no earlier than one day after the skill instructional period. For example, skills taught at meetings should be tested and signed off at the following meeting. Any skills taught on Scout outings may be tested the following day or at the next patrol meeting.

Aaronic Priesthood Support

- Insist that there is two-deep leadership associated with all eleven-year-old Scouting activities. Provide back-up if needed.
- If the leader of the eleven-year-old Scout patrol is a woman, arrange for males to supervise overnight camping experiences for these young men.
- Encourage Scout training for the EYOS leaders (Fast Start, This is Scouting, Position Specific, Outdoor training, Wood Badge, and roundtables.)
- Set the goal that the boys advance to First Class by age twelve.
- Encourage leaders to introduce merit badges, by pursuing a limited number of merit badges (perhaps 2 or 3 per year) in their meetings or activities.
- Provide training to their patrol leaders.
- Promote the full uniform for boys of their patrol.
- Assist EYOS leaders to develop their own program plan and calendar by adapting troop program planning methodologies.
- During months where the eleven-year-old Scouts are not camping, encourage the calendaring of a monthly day camp or an outdoor activity such as a hike.
- Invite EYOS leaders to troop committee meetings to report their plans and needs. Consider their needs for support equally with the other patrols in the troop.
- Encourage regular meetings of the eleven-year-old patrol, to keep up the Scouting momentum in the year between Cub Scouts and Young Men.
- Include needs of the EYOS program in troop fund-raising.
- Invite the Scoutmaster to attend eleven-year-old patrol meetings to get acquainted with these young men and encourage them in Scouting.
- Set standards for advancement record-keeping for the EYOS (use an online program or the Individual Scout Record form and keep an accurate record of over-night camps, service hours, and positions held by each boy).
- Advancement, activities, attendance, and leadership can be tracked online with Troopmaster (or a similar computer program). Information is transferred from Packmaster eliminating the need to enter the Scouts personal information and maintaining his Cub Scout achievements.
- Provide Boy Scouts who hold the Aaronic Priesthood to mentor and welcome the EYOS.
- Schedule boards of review when needed for advancement by EYOS.
- The EYOS leader holds Scoutmaster Conferences for advancement, introduces the Scouts to boards of review, and presents awards.
- EYOS should participate equally in courts of honor as part of the troop. Note: A rank requirement is to participate in a flag ceremony during a court of honor

Official BSA Policies

Boy Scout Policy on Advancement

Clause 5 – Basis for Advancement. The Boy Scout requirements for ranks shall be the basis for the Scout's advancement. There shall be four steps in Boy Scout advancement procedure: learning, testing, reviewing, and recognition.

Clause 6 – Ranks. There shall be the following ranks in Boy Scouting: Tenderfoot, Second Class, First Class, Star, Life, and Eagle. The requirements shall be authorized by the Executive Board and set forth in official Scouting publications. Eagle Palms may also be awarded on the basis of requirements authorized by the Executive Board and set forth in official Scouting publications.

Clause 7 – Responsibility of the Troop Committee. It shall be the responsibility of the troop committee, under the leadership and guidance of the local council, to make sure that the program of the troop is conducted in such a way that Scouts have an opportunity to advance on the basis of the four steps outlined in Clause 5.

Four Steps of Advancement

A Boy Scout advances from Tenderfoot to Eagle by doing things with his patrol and on his own. He advances by taking advantage of opportunities provided him.

1. **The Boy Scout learns.** A Scout learns by doing. He grows in ability to do his part as a member of the patrol and the troop. As he develops knowledge and skill, he teaches others; and in this way he begins to develop leadership.

2. **The Boy Scout is tested.** A Scout is tested on rank requirements by his patrol leader, Scoutmaster, assistant Scoutmaster, a troop committee member, or a member of his troop. The Scoutmaster maintains a list of those qualified to test and to pass-off.

3. **The Boy Scout is reviewed.** After a Scout has completed all requirements for a rank, he has a board of review. For Tenderfoot, Second Class, First Class, Star, Life, and Eagle Palms, the review is conducted by members of the troop committee. The Eagle Scout board of review is conducted in accordance with local council procedures.

4. **The Boy Scout is recognized.** When the board of review has certified a boy's advancement, he deserves to receive recognition as soon as possible. This should be done at a ceremony at the next troop meeting. The certificate for his new rank may be presented later at a formal court of honor.

Boy Scout Aims

The Boy Scout advancement program is subtle. It places a series of challenges in front of a Scout in a manner that is fun and educational. As Scouts meet these challenges, they achieve the aims of Boy Scouting.

One of the greatest needs of young men is confidence. There are three kinds of confidence that young men need: in themselves, in peers, and in leaders.

Educators and counselors agree that the best way to build confidence is through measurement. Self-confidence is developed by measuring up to a challenge or a standard. Peer confidence develops when the same measuring system is used for everyone -- when all must meet the same challenge to receive equal recognition. Confidence in leaders comes about when there is consistency in measuring -- when leaders use a single standard of fairness.

No council, district, unit, or individual has the authority to add to or subtract from any advancement requirement. A Boy Scout badge recognizes what a young man is able to do; it is not just a reward for what he has done.

Standards for joining a Boy Scout troop and for advancement are listed in the latest printing of the Boy Scout Handbook and in the current Boy Scout Requirements book.

Advancement accommodates the three aims of Scouting: citizenship, growth in moral strength and character, and mental and physical development. The program is designed to provide the Boy Scout with a chance to achieve the aims of Scouting. As a Scout advances, he is measured and grows in confidence and self-reliance.

When a badge and certificate are awarded to a Boy Scout to recognize that he has achieved a rank, they represent that a young man has:

- Been an active participant in his troop and patrol.
- Demonstrated living the Scout Oath (Promise) and Law in his daily life.
- Met the other requirements and/or earned the merit badges for the rank.
- Participated in a Scoutmaster conference.
- Satisfactorily appeared before a board of review.

In the advanced ranks (Star, Life, and Eagle), the badge represents that the young man has also:

- Served in a position of responsibility in the troop.
- Performed service to others.

Age Requirements

Boy Scout awards are for young men not yet eighteen years old. Any registered Boy Scout or Varsity Scout may earn merit badges, badges of rank, and Eagle Palms until his 18th birthday. Youth members with special needs may work towards rank advancement after they are eighteen.

Troop Advancement Goals

The Scoutmaster is in charge of advancement in the troop. It is necessary that the Scoutmaster understand the purpose of the advancement program and the importance it has in the development of the Scouts in the troop. The troop's program must provide advancement opportunities. By participating in the troop program, the Scout will meet requirements for rank advancement.

The troop's unit commissioner and the district advancement committee can play an important part in explaining advancement and helping the Scoutmaster utilize the advancement program in the troop program, making it exciting to the Scouts in the troop.

It is important that the troop committee and the Scoutmaster set an advancement goal for the year. When reviewed monthly by the troop committee, Scouts will recognize the importance of Scout advancement.

Troops should conduct boards of review for Scouts who are not advancing. A minimum of four formal courts of honor a year (one every three months) should be held to formally recognize the Scouts in the troop.

Presentation of merit badges and rank badges should not wait for a court of honor; awards and badges should be presented at the next meeting after they are earned, then Scouts are recognized again at a formal court of honor. Families attend the courts of honor just as they did the Cub Scout pack meeting.

Scoutmaster Conferences

One of the most enjoyable experiences of being an EYOS leader is the opportunity for a Scout and his leader to sit down and visit together.

In large troops, Scoutmasters occasionally assign this responsibility to assistant Scoutmasters or members of the troop committee; but this is unfortunate, because most Scoutmasters feel that this is truly the opportunity to get to know the Scout and help him chart his course in life.

The EYOS leader holds Scoutmaster Conferences with the Scouts in the EYOS patrol. A good conference should be unhurried. It helps the Scout evaluate his accomplishments and to set new goals with his EYOS leader. This can be accomplished at a troop meeting, camping trip, or in the Scout's home. Remember to always follow Youth Protection guidelines by holding a Scoutmaster conference in view of other adults and youth.

Goal setting by the Scout makes it possible for the EYOS leader to help the Scout with his weaknesses and encourage him to use his strengths.

All through the ranks, it is rewarding for the EYOS leader to observe the Scout grow in responsibility and maturity.

Record Keeping

Each troop is responsible for keeping its own records and reporting advancement to the local council service center. If this is done on an Advancement Report form, one copy is kept by the troop and two are sent to the council with an order for badges and awards. It is best that this form be submitted at least monthly so that troop records remain current and Scouts are able to receive their awards quickly after earning them. Awards cannot be purchased or awarded until the Advancement Report has been filed with the council office.

Troopmaster, an online computer program, tracks advancements and activities eliminating the need to use multi-part forms. At the discretion of the local council, computer-generated advancement reports may be used.

EYOS Program Planning Review

The basic information for planning and conducting EYOS patrol meetings and activities can be found in The Scoutmaster Handbook, the Boy Scout Handbook, Troop Program Resources, the Guide to Safe Scouting, and the (LDS) Scouting Handbook.

- Boys join the Boy Scouts when they turn eleven. Boys enter the program at any time in that year and work on rank advancement with the patrol, but they advance individually.
- Even on the three troop campouts, until boys turn twelve, it is recommended that their fathers, or male family members, camp with them. Boys can pass-off requirements on hikes and other activities planned throughout the year.
- Eleven-year-old Scouts attend a day camp planned by the stake, district, or council rather than attend the council week-long summer camp.
- Scout campouts are planned so the boys are home on Sunday.
- Because many of the units are small, stake activities provide fellowship with a larger group of boys.

Safety First

In conducting activities, the EYOS leadership must maintain adequate supervision and assure the proper use of materials. Be careful and remember: Safety must always come first!

Refer to the latest printing of the Guide to Safe Scouting, No 34426B, for information on guidelines relating to the many activities in which the EYOS patrol participates. There are several online training modules available on safety topics related to Scouting.

- Physical Wellness
- Safe Swim Defense
- Safety Afloat
- Climb on Safely
- Trek Safely
- Weather Hazards

To access online training, go to www.MyScouting.org.

EYOS Activities

- **EYOS Camp:** A day camp summer program for 1st year Boy Scouts to learn and demonstrate proficiency in outdoor sills and safety. The program may include water safety, cooking, fires, knots, lashing, knife care, service, and other related outdoor requirements for Tenderfoot, Second Class, and First Class ranks. EYOS Scouts can attend three separate overnight campouts with the Boy Scout troop during the year but they are not invited to attend long-term campouts with the troop.

- **Long-term Camp:** When the Scout is twelve, he attends long-term camping; however, it is recommended that fathers continue to participate in activities and attend with their sons. Scouting activities are designed to support the family.

- Eleven year old boys may participate in three one-night camps a year. These overnight campouts may be held with the ward's Boy Scout troop. The eleven-year-old Scout is part of the troop and the leader is an Assistant Scoutmaster. The Church provides an EYOS leader patch that can be purchased with other Primary materials.

Patrol Meetings

Include the following in the patrol meetings:
- Discussion of present and upcoming events.
- Things they need to do.
- Minutes of last meeting.
- Skills taught.
- End with a fun game and a brief closing ceremony.

Order of the Arrow

"The Order of the Arrow (OA) is Scouting's national honor society. It supports the teachings of the Church regarding cheerful service and brotherhood. Troops and teams may hold elections for their youth, and adults can be recommended for membership and participate as well. Each troop and team should have an active OA Troop or Team representative. Unit leaders should encourage all Arrowmen to stay active in their lodge."

Scouting & The Church of Jesus Christ of Latter-day Saints, LDS Relationships—BSA, page 10.

Tips for Success

Training

Leaders begin training by completing **Youth Protection** then **Boy Scout Fast Start** online. It is recommended that **This is Scouting** and **Position-Specific** training be completed during the first year; the sooner the better. Both are offered online and may also be offered by the council or district. Adults and youth will benefit from a fully trained leader with less frustration and a higher level of satisfaction from the calling. Additional training that is offered by the council includes **Scoutmaster Specific** and **Outdoor Leader Skills**. District roundtables provide continual up-to-date training and important information about both district and council activities and programs.

Parental Involvement

It is important to have two adult leaders, "two-deep leadership," for all outings and activities. Parents should be involved and encouraged to lend expertise to the program in their areas of interest. Each parent can contribute and should be invited to participate and use their skills. IMPORTANT: All parents who work with the boys should be BSA registered and complete Youth Protection Training.

Program Planning

An EYOS program plan that illustrates a rotating calendar is available online at www.LDS-Scouting.org. To achieve First Class before each boy turns twelve, the annual plan is organized to repeat the requirements for Tenderfoot, Second Class, and First Class several times throughout the year. The plan can be altered based on the birthdays of the boys in the patrol but it provides a guide to cover all requirements. Boys are taught leadership skills and encouraged to help plan activities and contribute ideas. They write a code of conduct and help discipline the patrol.

Participation

The boys and parents who participate get the most out of Scouting. It is important that boys understand that they are responsible for their own advancement. A well-planned program will provide the boys with the opportunities they need to advance. The boys work the plan to achieve their goals.

Success

Leadership is learned and developed. The EYOS program is successful if the leaders are trained, the patrol meetings are interesting, and the leaders understand eleven-year-old boys. The plan should be flexible and fun. Boys learn good values and worthy skills along their way to becoming adults.

LDS Guide to Scouting in the Primary

EYOS Program Instructions

The EYOS meeting plans, "program helps" for the EYOS leader, are coordinated to help every boy achieve First Class by his twelfth birthday. The program covers the basic requirements for Tenderfoot, Second Class, and First Class plus matches games and Scoutmaster's minutes to the skills instructions. The Boy Scout Handbook is referenced as assignments for each skill so boys are prepared for the patrol meeting.

Each meeting covers requirements for all three ranks, but the program should be customized to meet the needs of the boys as they enter the program on their birthday. Most EYOS patrols are small making it an easy task to modify and adapt the program. Monitoring the boys' progress in Troopmaster or a similar online tracking tool is a good way to ensure that the boys are progressing at the desired rate.

The page numbers listed in the *Gathering, Opening, Skills Instruction*, and *Assignment* sections of the meeting plans in this guide refer to the **2009 Boy Scout Handbook.**

The page numbers in the *Scoutmaster's Minute* and *Closing Game* sections of the meeting plans in this guide refers to the **Troop Program Resources**.

The EYOS meeting plans provide ideas for patrol meetings, activities (ten are required every year), advancement requirements, and other Boy Scout activities. They are suggestions and do not reflect a required order in achieving the Tenderfoot, Second Class, and First Class ranks.

Troop Program Resources (Scoutmaster's Minutes, Games, Ceremonies, Interfaith Worship Services, Quotes from Baden-Powell, and Clip Art) are available as PDF files on www.scouting.org.

A direct link to the Troop Program Resources is listed below.
www.scouting.org/scoutsource/BoyScouts/Resources/Troop%20Program%20Resources.aspx.

Additional ideas are available in the **Scoutmaster Handbook**, at roundtables, in **Scouting Magazine**, and other documents such as the **Troop Program Feature**s.

Available as PDF files on www.scouting.org **Troop Program Features I – III** can be downloaded and used to plan effective meetings.

www.scouting.org/scoutsource/BoyScouts/Resources/Troop%20Program%20Features%20Vol,-d-,%20I%20-%20III.aspx

The initial Scoutmaster conference with the Scoutmaster and EYOS leaders occurs immediately prior to joining the EYOS patrol. At that meeting the Scoutmasters review pages 12 – 41 in the **Boy Scout Handbook** with the new Scout and set goals that the new Boy Scout can work on.

The second Scoutmaster conference covers *Leadership* on pages 46 – 63. At this point the boy may have questions and concerns that the Scoutmaster can resolve.

January EYOS Meeting Plan

	Week One	Week Two	Week Three	Week Four
Before the Meeting	PLC Meeting	PLC Meeting	PLC Meeting	PLC Meeting
Gathering [a]	Review Scout Oath, Law, Motto, Slogan, Patrol Spirit, Outdoor Code 16-41	Physical Best 95-101: Push-ups, Pull-ups, Sit-ups, Standing long jump, 1/4-mile walk/run	Review Merit Badges and Sign-off Requirements	Review and Sign-off Knots and Lashing
Opening [a]	Flag Ceremony 68-76	Flag Ceremony	Flag Ceremony	Flag Ceremony
Skills Instruction [a]	**Advancement** Review Merit Badge Clinic and preparation for merit badges Review Scout Handbook – Merit Badge Requirements	**Camping/Hiking** Care, sharpening, and use of the knife, saw, and ax Prepare fuel for fire Use of fire / stove Light fire / stove	**Knots / Lashing** Demonstrate how to whip and fuse the ends of a rope. Demonstrate that you know how to tie the following knots and tell what their uses are: two half hitches and the taut-line hitch.	**First Aid** Demonstrate the Heimlich maneuver. Show first aid for: • Cuts/ scratches • Blisters – hand/foot • Minor burns / scalds • Bites or stings of insects and ticks • Poisonous snakebite • Nosebleed • Frostbite; sunburn
Patrol Meeting				
Closing Game [b]	Bucketball – 31	Fuzz-stick Relay – 41	Knot Hoop Relay – 47	Remedies – 56
Scoutmaster's Minute [b]	Aim so High you'll Never be Bored – 6	Don't Be Afraid to Fail – 5	One Person Can Make a Difference – 5	The Slim Margin of Success – 5
Assignment [a]	48-51	253, 301, 325, 401-408, 414-415	380-385	134-143, 148-153
After the Meeting	Scoutmaster Conference	Scoutmaster Conference	Scoutmaster Conference	Scoutmaster Conference

Activity: Merit Badge Clinic

a. 2009 Boy Scout Handbook   b. Troop Program Resources

February EYOS Meeting Plan

	Week One	Week Two	Week Three	Week Four
Before the Meeting	PLC Meeting	PLC Meeting	PLC Meeting	PLC Meeting
Gathering [a]	Review and sign-off First Aid and Scout Oath, etc.	Physical Best 95-101: Push-ups, Pull-ups, Sit-ups, Standing long jump, 1/4-mile walk/run	Review and Sign-off on Swimming Requirements	Review and Sign-off on Knots and Lashing
Opening [a]	Flag Ceremony 68-76	Flag Ceremony	Flag Ceremony	Flag Ceremony
Skills Instruction [a]	**Citizenship** Participate in a school, community, or troop program on the dangers of using drugs, alcohol, and tobacco, etc. ***** Special Note: Discuss your participation in the program with your family.**	**Swimming** Tell what precautions must be taken for a safe swim. Tell what precautions must be taken for a safe trip afloat. Review Swimming Requirements for 2nd and 1st Class	**Knots / Lashing** Discuss when you should and should not use lashings. Demonstrate tying the timber hitch and clove hitch and use in square, shear, and diagonal lashings. Use lashing to make a useful camp gadget.	**First Aid** Show "hurry" cases Personal first aid kit • Object in the eye • Bite rabid animal • Puncture wounds • Serious burns • Heat exhaustion • Shock • Heatstroke, etc.
Patrol Meeting				
Closing Game [b]	Stepping Stones – 26	Water Dodgeball – 71	Clove-Hitch Race – 34	Human Ladder – 24
Scoutmaster's Minute [b]	A Scout is Clean – 8	Water World – 6	A Bicycle – 6	Aptitude and Attitude – 7
Assignment [a]	113-119	180-201	392-401	1124-133, 140-151
After the Meeting	Scoutmaster Conference	Scoutmaster Conference	Scoutmaster Conference	Scoutmaster Conference

Activity: Winter Swim (Second and First Class requirements)

a. 2009 Boy Scout Handbook b. Troop Program Resources

LDS Guide to Scouting in the Primary

March EYOS Meeting Plan

	Week One	Week Two	Week Three	Week Four
Before the Meeting	PLC Meeting	PLC Meeting	PLC Meeting	PLC Meeting
Gathering [a]	Review and sign-off First Aid and Scout Oath, etc.	Physical Best 95-101: Push-ups, Pull-ups, Sit-ups, Standing long jump, 1/4-mile walk/run	Review Leave No Trace Principles – Travel and Camp on Durable Surfaces, 248	Review and sign-off Hiking
Opening [a]	Flag Ceremony 68-76	Flag Ceremony	Flag Ceremony	Flag Ceremony
Skills Instruction [a]	**Citizenship** Participate in an approved service project (minimum of one hour).	**Camping/Hiking** Explain safe hiking; what to do if lost. Demonstrate how a compass, orient a map, explain symbols Demonstrate directions during day and night without a compass.	**Cooking** • Four basic food groups, store, and prepare food • Plan a patrol menu to meets nutrition needs • Cost and food amounts needed to feed patrol • Pans, etc. to cook and serve meals • Safe handling of food and dispose garbage	**Knots / Lashing** Demonstrate tying the bowline knot **First Aid** • Demonstrate bandage • Transport from smoky room • Sprained ankle • Heart attack • Explain CPR • Poisoning
Patrol Meeting				
Closing Game [b]	Two-Person Square-Knot Tying – 70	Getting Your Bearings – 42	Flapjack-Flipping Relay – 40	Arm-Sling Relay – 28
Scoutmaster's Minute [b]	Giving – 9	Which Path? – 11	Hot Cocoa – 10	Reach Higher – 6
Assignment [a]	77-79, 84	262-269, 282-283, 361-375	102-107, 314-343	156-177, 388-289
After the Meeting	Scoutmaster Conference	Scoutmaster Conference	Scoutmaster Conference	Scoutmaster Conference

Activity: Five-mile Hike (compass and map, orienteering)

a. 2009 Boy Scout Handbook   b. Troop Program Resources

April EYOS Meeting Plan

	Week One	Week Two	Week Three	Week Four
Before the Meeting	PLC Meeting	PLC Meeting	PLC Meeting	PLC Meeting
Gathering [a]	Review and sign-off First Aid and Scout Oath, etc.	Physical Best 95-101: Push-ups, Pull-ups, Sit-ups, Standing long jump, 1/4-mile walk/run	Review and sign-off Campcrafts Skills	Review and Sign-off plants and animals
Opening [a]	Flag Ceremony 68-76	Flag Ceremony	Flag Ceremony	Flag Ceremony
Skills Instruction [a]	**Citizenship** Visit and discuss a leader (elected official, judge, attorney, civil servant, principal, teacher) your Constitutional rights and obligations as a U.S. citizen.	**Camping/Hiking** Care, sharpening, and use of the knife, saw, and ax. Prepare fuel for fire. Use of fire / stove. Light fire / stove.	**Community** Identify poisonous plants and animals. Identify ten animals. Identify ten plants.	**First Aid** Demonstrate the Heimlich maneuver. Show first aid for: • Cuts/ scratches • Blisters – hand/foot • Minor burns or scalds • Bites or stings of insects and ticks • Poisonous snakebite • Nosebleed • Frostbite; sunburn
Patrol Meeting				
Closing Game [b]	Famous Visitors – 38	Fire Bucket Relay – 38	Nature Scavenger Hunt – 52	First-Aid Problems – 39
Scoutmaster's Minute [b]	Our Flag – 13	Matches – 12	Goose Story – 11	Being Clean – 14
Assignment [a]	80-83	253, 301, 325, 414-415	138-143, 206-231	134-143, 148-153
After the Meeting	Scoutmaster Conference	Scoutmaster Conference	Scoutmaster Conference	Scoutmaster Conference

Activity: Public Meeting

Activity: Outdoor Activity (fuel and stoves)

a. 2009 Boy Scout Handbook   b. Troop Program Resources

May EYOS Meeting Plan

	Week One	Week Two	Week Three	Week Four
Before the Meeting	PLC Meeting	PLC Meeting	PLC Meeting	PLC Meeting
Gathering [a]	Review and Sign-off First Aid	Discuss Leave No Trace – Dispose of Waste Properly 249-250	Review and Sign-off on Camping / Cooking Requirements	Review and Sign-off Knots and Lashing
Opening [a]	Flag Ceremony 68-76	Flag Ceremony	Flag Ceremony	Flag Ceremony
Skills Instruction [a]	**Camping/Hiking** Present properly dressed, before going on overnight camping trip. Show camping gear, how to pack and carry it. Discuss selecting your patrol site and sleep in a tent that you pitched.	**Camping/Hiking** On campout, assist in cooking a patrol meal On campout cook over an open fire one hot breakfast or lunch On campout supervise/ prepare 3 meals. Pray. Supervise cleanup	**Knots / Lashing** Discuss lashings Demonstrate tying the timber hitch and clove hitch and use in square, shear, and diagonal lashings. Use lashing to make a useful camp gadget.	**First Aid** Show "hurry" cases Personal 1st aid kit • Object in the eye • Bite rabid animal • Puncture wounds • Serious burns • Heat exhaustion • Shock • Heatstroke, etc.
Patrol Meeting				
Closing Game [b]	The Leaking BackPack – 48	Hockey Steal-the-Bacon – 43	Get 'em Up – 41	Kim's Game – 47
Scoutmaster's Minute [b]	Whose Job Is It? – 16	Why Are You In Scouting? – 10	Can't To Can! – 6	Symbols – 6
Assignment [a]	270-276, 290-306	326-343	386-400	124-133, 140-151
After the Meeting	Scoutmaster Conference	Scoutmaster Conference	Scoutmaster Conference	Scoutmaster Conference

Activity: Campout

a. 2009 Boy Scout Handbook   b. Troop Program Resources

June EYOS Meeting Plan

	Week One	Week Two	Week Three	Week Four
Before the Meeting	PLC Meeting	PLC Meeting	PLC Meeting	EYOS Camp* Pack clothes and camping gear
Gathering (a)	Review and Sign-off First Aid	Review Advancement and set goals for Camp	Review Requirements for Totin' Chip 409, Campfire 410-414, Outdoor Code 28, 245	Pitch tent Cook one meal Cook, cleanup Whip / fuse rope Half/taut-line hitch
Opening (a)	Flag Ceremony 68-76	Flag Ceremony	Flag Ceremony	Safe hiking American flag Buddy system
Skills Instruction (a)	**Camping/Hiking** Review pack clothes and camping gear Explain safe hiking; what to do if lost. Identify poisonous plants and animals Identify ten animals Identify ten plants	**Camping/Hiking** Demonstrate how a compass, orient a map, explain symbols Review directions during the day and at night Orienteering course Plan three meals Cost and food Utensils needed Safe food storage Dispose of garbage	**Leave No Trace** • Plan Ahead and Prepare • Travel and Camp on Durable Surfaces • Dispose of Waste Property • Leave What You Find • Minimize Campfire Impacts • Respect Wildlife • Be Considerate of Other Visitors	Poisonous plants Compass and map 5-mile hike Select site and tent Knife, saw, and ax Tinder, kindling Fire and stove Cook one hot meal Flag ceremony Service project Wild animals Personal 1st aid kit Safe swim Swim 25 ft and back Water rescue Orienteering Menu three meals
Patrol Meeting				
Closing Game (b)	Nature Memory Hunt –52	Blindfold Compass walk –30	Night Crossing – 25	Cost and food Utensils needed Safe food storage and Disposal
Scoutmaster's Minute (b)	Two Knapsacks –11	Our Spiritual Compass –15	A Scout is Considerate – 13	patrol cook, prayer, cleanup Native plants Lashings Timber/clove hitch
Assignment (a)	138-143, 206-231, 262-283, 298-299	102-107, 314-342, 346-375	244-257	
After the Meeting	Scoutmaster Conference	Scoutmaster Conference	Scoutmaster Conference	Lash camp gadget Bowline knot Safe trip afloat BSA swimmer test Victim rescue

Activity: EYOS Camp

a. 2009 Boy Scout Handbook   b. Troop Program Resources

LDS Guide to Scouting in the Primary

July EYOS Meeting Plan

	Week One	Week Two	Week Three	Week Four
Before the Meeting	4th of July Sunrise Flag Ceremony	PLC Meeting	PLC Meeting	PLC Meeting
Gathering [a]		Physical Best 95-101: Push-ups, Pull-ups, Sit-ups, Standing long jump, 1/4-mile walk/run	Review Requirements and Sign-off for Tenderfoot, 2nd Class, 1st Class	Review and Sign-off Knots and Lashing
Opening [a]	Flag Ceremony 68-76	Flag Ceremony	Flag Ceremony	Flag Ceremony
Skills Instruction [a]		**Camp Review** Review progress at camp and complete advancement records. Scoutmaster Conference with each boy Plan summer activities	**Knots / Lashing** Review all knots and lashing Square Knot Two half hitches Taut-line hitch Timber hitch Clove hitch Bowline knot Square lashing Shear lashing Diagonal lashing	**First Aid** Demonstrate the Heimlich maneuver. Show first aid for: • Cuts/ scratches • Blisters – hand/foot • Minor burns / scalds • Bites or stings of insects and ticks • Poisonous snakebite • Nosebleed • Frostbite; sunburn
Patrol Meeting				
Closing Game [b]		Fitness Medley Relay – 39	Blindman's Knots – 30	Grand Prix Game – 42
Scoutmaster's Minute [b]		The Scout Salute and Handshake – 12	Everybody's Canoe – 13	The Carnival – 12
Assignment [a]		286-311	382-401	134-143, 148-153
After the Meeting		Scoutmaster Conference	Scoutmaster Conference	Scoutmaster Conference

Activity: July 4th Flag Ceremony / Sunrise Flag Ceremony

a. 2009 Boy Scout Handbook   b. Troop Program Resources

August EYOS Meeting Plan

	Week One	Week Two	Week Three	Week Four
Before the Meeting	PLC Meeting	PLC Meeting	PLC Meeting	PLC Meeting
Gathering [a]	Review and Sign-off First Aid and Scout Spirit	Physical Best 95-101: Push-ups, Pull-ups, Sit-ups, Standing long jump, 1/4-mile walk/run	Review Leave No Trace Principles – Leave What You Find, Respect Wildlife, 251-252, 254-255	Sign-off service project, hiking and orienteering
Opening [a]	Flag Ceremony 68-76	Flag Ceremony	Flag Ceremony	Flag Ceremony
Skills Instruction [a]	**Faith in God** Review the requirements for the Faith in God Award and discuss the Aaronic Priesthood	**Camping/Hiking** Explain safe hiking; what to do if lost. Demonstrate how a compass, orient a map, explain symbols. Demonstrate directions during day and night without a compass.	**Citizenship** Participate in an approved (minimum of one hour) service project. Possible project – pick up trash along a roadway or in a public park while hiking.	**Knots / Lashing** Demonstrate tying the bowline knot **First Aid** • Demonstrate bandage • Transport from smoky room • Sprained ankle • Heart attack • Explain CPR • Poisoning
Patrol Meeting				
Closing Game [b]	Everybody Up –24	Direction-Finding Relay –37	Newspaper Good Turn –53	Bandage Relay – 29
Scoutmaster's Minute [b]	We Make A Difference – 16	Footprints – 5	A Quiet Hero – 14	The Golden Windows – 12
Assignment [a]	430	262-269, 277-283, 346-375	77-79, 84	156-177, 388-289
After the Meeting	Scoutmaster Conference	Scoutmaster Conference	Scoutmaster Conference	Scoutmaster Conference

a. 2009 Boy Scout Handbook   b. Troop Program Resources

September EYOS Meeting Plan

	Week One	Week Two	Week Three	Week Four
Before the Meeting	PLC Meeting	PLC Meeting	PLC Meeting	PLC Meeting
Gathering [a]	Review and Sign-off First Aid and Scout Spirit	Physical Best 95-101: Push-ups, Pull-ups, Sit-ups, Standing long jump, 1/4-mile walk/run	Review and Sign-off Hiking and Orienteering	Review and Sign-off Campcraft Skills
Opening [a]	Flag Ceremony 68-76	Flag Ceremony	Flag Ceremony	Flag Ceremony
Skills Instruction [a]	**Citizenship** Visit and discuss a leader (elected official, judge, attorney, civil servant, principal, teacher) your Constitutional rights and obligations as a U.S. citizen.	**Camping/Hiking** Explain safe hiking; what to do if lost. Demonstrate how a compass, orient a map, explain symbols Demonstrate directions during day and night without a compass.	**Cooking** Four basic food groups, store, and prepare food Plan a patrol menu to meets nutrition needs Cost and food amounts needed to feed patrol Pans, etc. to cook and serve these meals Safe handling of food and dispose garbage	**First Aid** Demonstrate the Heimlich maneuver. Show first aid for: • Cuts/ scratches • Blisters – hand/foot • Minor burns / scalds • Bites or stings of insects and ticks • Poisonous snakebite • Nosebleed • Frostbite; sunburn
Patrol Meeting				
Closing Game [b]	Capture the Flag – 32	Catch-the-Snapper – 33	What's Cooking – 72	Newspaper Crimpling – 52
Scoutmaster's Minute [b]	Loyalty – 7	Game of Cards – 7	A Good Turn – 18	Be Prepared For What? – Page 9
Assignment [a]	80-83	262-269, 277-283, 346-375	102-107, 314-343	134-143, 148-153
After the Meeting	Scoutmaster Conference	Scoutmaster Conference	Scoutmaster Conference	Scoutmaster Conference

Activity: Fall Orienteering Hike – Hike / Bike / Repel

a. 2009 Boy Scout Handbook   b. Troop Program Resources

LDS Guide to Scouting in the Primary

October EYOS Meeting Plan

	Week One	Week Two	Week Three	Week Four
Before the Meeting	PLC Meeting	PLC Meeting	PLC Meeting	PLC Meeting
Gathering [a]	Review and Sign-off First Aid and Scout Spirit	Physical Best 95-101: Push-ups, Pull-ups, Sit-ups, Standing long jump, 1/4-mile walk/run	Review Leave No Trace Principles – Plan Ahead and Prepare, 247 Be Considerate of Other Visitors, 256	Review and Sign-off on Camping / Cooking Requirements
Opening [a]	Flag Ceremony 68-76	Flag Ceremony	Flag Ceremony	Flag Ceremony
Skills Instruction [a]	Camping/Hiking Care, sharpening, and use of the knife, saw, and ax Prepare fuel for fire Use of fire / stove Light fire / stove	Camping/Hiking Present properly dressed, before going on overnight camping trip. Show camping gear, how to pack and carry it. Discuss selecting your patrol site and sleep in a tent that you pitched.	Camping/Hiking On campout, assist in cooking a patrol meal On campout cook over an open fire one hot breakfast or lunch On campout supervise/ prepare 3 meals. Pray. Supervise cleanup	First Aid Show "hurry" cases Personal 1st aid kit • Object in the eye • Bite rabid animal • Puncture wounds • Serious burns • Heat exhaustion • Shock • Heatstroke, etc.
Patrol Meeting				
Closing Game [b]	Nail-Driving Relay – 51	Jump the Shot – 46	Lost Quiz –50	First-aid Baseball – 38
Scoutmaster's Minute [b]	Losing Your Temper – 18	Happiness – 8	Persistence – 8	Trick or Treat – 8
Assignment [a]	402-415	270-276, 290-306	326-343	124-133, 140-151
After the Meeting	Scoutmaster Conference	Scoutmaster Conference	Scoutmaster Conference	Scoutmaster Conference

Activity: Campout

a. 2009 Boy Scout Handbook   b. Troop Program Resources

November EYOS Meeting Plan

	Week One	Week Two	Week Three	Week Four
Before the Meeting	PLC Meeting	PLC Meeting	PLC Meeting	
Gathering [a]	Review and Sign-off First Aid and Scout Spirit	Physical Best 95-101: Push-ups, Pull-ups, Sit-ups, Standing long jump, 1/4-mile walk/run	Review Tenderfoot, 2nd Class, 1st Class	
Opening [a]	Flag Ceremony 68-76	Flag Ceremony	Flag Ceremony	Thanksgiving
Skills Instruction [a]	**Citizenship** Participate in a school, community, or troop program on the dangers of using drugs, alcohol, and tobacco, etc. ***** Special Note: Discuss your participation in the program with your family.**	**Service Project** Participate in an approved (minimum of one hour) service project. Possible project – food pantry, toys for tots, visit old folks home	**Knots / Lashing** Demonstrate tying the bowline knot **First Aid** • Demonstrate bandage • Transport from smoky room • Sprained ankle • Heart attack • Explain CPR • Poisoning	
Patrol Meeting		Plan on Funding Camp Program		
Closing Game [b]	Mow the Man Down – 51	Scouting History – 59	Lifeline Relay – 48	
Scoutmaster's Minute [b]	Bravery – 8	A Good Turn – 10	Thanksgiving – 7	
Assignment [a]	113-119	77-89	156-177, 388-289	
After the Meeting	Scoutmaster Conference	Scoutmaster Conference	Scoutmaster Conference	

Activity: Personal Fitness Challenge @ Sports Complex

a. 2009 Boy Scout Handbook   b. Troop Program Resources

December EYOS Meeting Plan

	Week One	Week Two	Week Three	Week Four
Before the Meeting	PLC Meeting	PLC Meeting	PLC Meeting	
Gathering [a]	Review and Sign-off First Aid and Scout Spirit	Physical Best 95-101: Push-ups, Pull-ups, Sit-ups, Standing long jump, 1/4-mile walk/run	Review and Sign-off on Knots and Lashing	Christmas
Opening [a]	Flag Ceremony 68-76	Flag Ceremony	Flag Ceremony	
Skills Instruction [a]	**Faith in God** Review the requirements for the Faith in God Award and discuss the Aaronic Priesthood	**Knots / Lashing** Discuss when you should and should not use lashings. Demonstrate tying the timber hitch and clove hitch and use in square, shear, and diagonal lashings. Use lashing to make a useful camp gadget.	**Advancement** Review Merit Badge Clinic and preparation for merit badges Review Scout Handbook – Merit Badge	
Patrol Meeting				
Closing Game [b]	Who Am I? – 73	Flagpole Raising – 40	Name the Merit Badge – 51	
Scoutmaster's Minute [b]	The High Cost of Getting Even – 10	Trim Your Sail – 8	Aim at Something High – 8	
Assignment [a]	430	380-400	Merit Badge selected	
After the Meeting	Scoutmaster Conference	Scoutmaster Conference	Scoutmaster Conference	

a. 2009 Boy Scout Handbook   b. Troop Program Resources

Sample EYOS Activities

Month	Activity	Sponsor	Location
January	Merit Badge Clinic	Stake	Stake Center
February	Winter Swim / Sports Challenge	Stake	Sport Center
March	Spring Compass (Hike)	Wards	Chapel
April	Campfire @ Forest Preserve	Scout troop	County Forest Preserve
May	Spring Campout	Ward	Father and Son
June	EYOS Camp	Stake	Camp Crown
July	Flag Ceremony	Ward	Ward Activity
August	Summer Activity	Ward	Ward Activity
September	Hike / Bike / Repel	Scout troop	Devil's Lake
October	Fall Campout	District / Council	TBD
November	Sports / Fitness	Wards	Libertyville Sport

In addition to activities correlated to advancement, the EYOS program includes Faith in God activities, service projects, and courts of honor. Boys in EYOS are given opportunities to live the gospel principles they learn in class on Sunday and at home and participate in activities that prepare them to receive the Aaronic Priesthood.

The unit's EYOS program should be adapted to meet the needs of the boys in the program and the activities available through the local district, council, wards, and stake. The program outlined above is a guide that provides examples of rotating activities so all EYOS achieve First Class before they turn twelve.

LDS Guide to Scouting in the Primary

Eleven-year-old Scout Review

When you plan an effective EYOS Program, consider these points:

- The first year a boy is in Boy Scouts is the most important and the most complex, so planning a successful program is a challenge for the EYOS leader. But it can be done and it is very rewarding!!

- A Troop Guide can provide a learning environment and assist the EYOS leader in maintaining the advancement records for each Scout.

- The program includes repetition of the skills instruction. Boys remember the basic skills longer if they repeat the instruction. If a Scout knows the skill, then he can be assigned to teach the skill to other Scouts, or the Scout can prepare a presentation to demonstrate his knowledge.

- Sample troop meeting plans provided in the Scoutmaster Handbook and published for first-year Scouts can be helpful but they may be designed around a monthly theme or focus on one skill. This works well for boys who join the patrol together at the end of their 5th grade and most expect the Scouts to attend summer camp when they are eleven. The program for EYOS requires more flexibility and a continual rotation of the skills during the first year.

- To earn the Second Class rank, the boy must attend five activities planned outside the patrol meeting, including stake activities, campouts, hikes, service projects, and local government board meetings. To earn the First Class rank, the boy must attend an additional five activities. That is a total of ten activities in one year!!

- Three of the activities must be campouts. It is important that all boys attend the campouts planned for spring, summer (which may be at a stake EYOS day camp), and fall. The campouts are spread out to achieve the goal that all boys receive their First Class rank by twelve.

- Like campouts, service projects are planned a couple times a year. A Second Class requirement includes a one-hour service project, such as, picking up trash along the road or assisting with an Eagle service project.

- Safe Swimming requirements are important but difficult to plan because of the need to go to a safe location to pass-off the requirements.

- There are four steps in the Scout Advancement Procedure: learn, test, review, recognize. Boys sign-off on requirements at least one week after skill instruction rather than at the same time they learn the skills.

- EYOS are recognized at the troop court of honor. A court of honor can be planned on the activity night during the months with a fifth week.

- Performing in the flag Ceremony is a Second Class requirement. If the EYOS patrol performs it at every troop court of honor, new boys will be able to pass-off the requirement.

Summary LDS Scouting

Summary LDS Guide to Scouting in the Primary

Scouting in the Church of Jesus Christ of Latter-day Saints follows guidelines from Church Headquarters in Salt Lake City. The 2011 Scouting Handbook for Church Units in the United States describes the Church's relationship to Cub Scouting and how to use the program as the youth program for boys eight – ten years old. It also explains the Boy Scouting program for boys eleven – eighteen. Although the aims of BSA and Church program are essentially the same, there are a couple differences in the implementation. Packs chartered by wards in the Church do not participate in Tiger Cubs nor do they participate in over-night camping even for Webelos. An all-day hike will meet the requirement for Arrow of Light. Boy Scout troops are cautioned not to travel or camp on Sunday. Funding is designed to ensure that all boys can participate in Scouting without placing a hardship of the families.

LDS Objective

Scouting activities provide boys with the opportunity to put into practice the gospel principles they learn at home and at Church.

LDS Methods

- Cub Scout meetings should be held preferably in the daytime at the meetinghouse, in a home, or in an outdoor setting.
- All Scout meetings and activities should open and close with prayer.
- Boys enter and advance in Scout programs by age.
- The Cub Scout program in the Church begins at age eight and does not support BSA programs for boys younger than eight; i.e. Tiger Cubs in the United States or Beavers in Canada.
- The Webelos program is one year with a focus on achieving the Webelos rank and Arrow of Light. A day hike rather than an overnight campout meets the Arrow of Light requirement.
- The stake registers all boys and young men ages eight through fifteen and young men sixteen and seventeen who are pursuing rank advancement or if the ward sponsors a Venturing Crew. Scout leaders are also registered through the stake funds.
- Boys who are not members are welcome to register with the ward's pack and are registered in the same way as members.
- The Church does not sponsor Scouting for girls or young women.
- Qualified adults, whether members of the Church or not, may hold Scouting positions. All must maintain the Church standards.
- Leaders are asked to serve in the role; however, families and parents are always welcomed to volunteer in many supportive roles.
- Members are set apart by a member of the bishopric; other leaders may receive a blessing from the bishopric.

LDS Guide to Scouting in the Primary

- Where leadership is limited, one committee may be called to service the Aaronic Priesthood and another Cub Scouts.
- Men or women can serve in Scout positions for Primary age boys (Cub Scouting and eleven-year-old Scouts) but only men are called to work directly with the Aaronic Priesthood young men. A woman can serve as the committee chairman.
- No Scout-sponsored overnight camping should be planned for boys less than eleven years.
- The ward should not observe Scout Sunday during a sacrament meeting.
- No hiking or camping on Sunday. Cub Scouts should not travel to or from camp on Sunday. Exceptions to camping on Sunday require special approval.
- **Faith in God** is the Cub Scout religious award. Boys complete requirements marked with a square knot in their **Faith in God** booklet.
- Leaders should follow the budget allowance guidelines to finance the Scouting program. It is important to turn in all receipts.
- Dues are not collected. All programs are paid out of the ward budget. Note: the ward budget is not used to buy uniforms, but it can be used to pay for leader training.
- Registration and unit chartering fees are paid from the stake general checking account.
- Boys' Life is paid for by the parents or from the ward budget.
- Cub Scout and Boy Scout awards and activity fees come from the ward budget.
- The Church encourages the participation in one annual day camp (district, stake, or council). It should be funded by the ward budget. If the ward does not have funds, then the participant's parents may be asked to pay for part or all of the camp. The inability to pay should not exclude a Cub Scout from attending day camp.
- Lack of personal funds should not prohibit participation.
- One fund raiser per year is permitted to purchase capital equipment and one fund raiser to pay for long-term camping.
- Tour plans should be filed with the bishop and the BSA council office following the council's guidelines.
- No activities should be planned for Monday evenings. The Church sets aside Monday evening for Family Home Evening. This is an activity that the family does together and is intended to strengthen the family unit.
- *"Training courses that require overnight activities should not be attended by mixed groups of adult men and women unless both genders have appropriate sleeping and personal care arrangements that are not in immediate proximity to each other. Where possible, leaders should attend training offered on days other than Sunday."* (Scouting Handbook, page 1.)

Contact Joanne Osmond at Jo@LDS-Scouting.com or (847)356-7550 for more information.

"Boys need lots of heroes like Lincoln and Washington. But they also need to have some heroes close by. They need to know some man of towering strength and basic integrity, personally. They need to meet them on the street, to hike and camp with them, to see them in close-to-home, everyday, down-to-earth situations; to feel close enough to them to ask questions and talk things over man-to-man with them."

"Boys Need Heroes Close By"

Spencer W. Kimball

Ensign, May 1976, p. 45, 47